A
WORLD
WITHOUT
WALL
STREET?

T0345591

THE FRENCH LIST

A WORLD WITHOUT WALL STREET?

François Morin

TRANSLATED BY KRZYSZTOF FIJALKOWSKI
AND MICHAEL RICHARDSON

LONDON NEW YORK CALCUTTA

The translators would like to thank Yoko Akashi and François Morin for their help with appropriate translations for some of the financial terms in the text.

This work is published via the Publication Assistance Programme Tagore, with the support of Institut Français en Inde/Ambassade de France en Inde.

Seagull Books, 2013

François Morin, *Un monde sans Wall Street?*
© Éditions du Seuil, 2011

English translation
© Michael Richardson and Krzysztof Fijalkowski, 2011

ISBN   978 0 8574 2 031 2

British Library Cataloguing-in-Publication Data
A catalogue record for this book is available from the British Library

Typeset and designed by Seagull Books, Calcutta, India
Printed and bound by Maple Press, York, Pennsylvania, USA

To Émile and Tom

'But we shall conquer, because we are Justice. There! You see that building in front of you ? You see it?'

'The Bourse?' said Saccard. 'Why, yes, of course I see it.'

'Well, it would be stupid to blow it up, because it would be rebuilt. Only I predict to you that it will go up of itself when the State has expropriated it, and have become the sole universal bank of the nation; and, who knows? Perhaps it will then serve as a public warehouse for our surplus wealth, as one of the storehouses where our grandchildren will find the necessary supply of luxury for their days of festivity.'

Emile Zola, *Money*

CONTENTS

I am entirely responsible for conceiving and writing this essay and therefore I alone assume its possible limits and imperfections.

Nevertheless, I would very much like to thank all those people with whom I have discussed this work and who have helped to clarify the analyses and ideas presented in it.

From the time the financial crisis unfolded and since my earlier work was published in 2006 in the series edited by Jacques Généreux, to whom I would like once more to give all my gratitude for his advice, I have been fortunate enough to have met with or been in contact with very many community or political leaders. Unfortunately I cannot mention them all, but I would especially like to thank Lionel Jospin, Jean Le Garrec, Jean-Luc Mélenchon, Jacques Cheminade and Jean-Claude Trichet for their observations or their assessment of the situation the crisis has created.

Meetings and discussions with scholars have been equally numerous and stimulating, especially with Michel Aglietta, Samir Amin, Olivier Brossard, Gabriel Colletis, Gilles Dostaler, Pierre Grou, François Houtart, Frédérique Lordon, Patrick Mignard, André Orléan, Éric Pineault, Dominique Plihon and Bruno Théret. I would like here to thank them all.

LIST OF ABBREVIATIONS

OECD	Organization for Economic Co-operation and Development
EMU	Economic and Monetary Union
OPE	Offre publique d'echange
OPA	Offre publique d'achat
AFEP	Association française d'économie politique
CAPM	Capital Asset Pricing Model
APT	Arbitrage Pricing Theory
CDS	Credit Default Swap
ILO	International Labour Organization
IPBES	Intergovernmental Science-Policy Platform on Biodiversity and Ecosystem Services
INSEE	Institut national de la statistique et des études économiques
ICAPM	Intertemporal Capital Asset Pricing Model

Why is the crisis still with us? Why has it continued in forms increasingly dangerous for our economic planet and for us citizens? Since August 2007, our leaders have been telling us (at intervals of around three weeks) that the worst of the financial crisis is behind us. Why have they been, and why are they still, so gravely mistaken?

The least dogmatic among them declare that they are acting in a pragmatic way in the face of a succession of events that were not at all predictable. For them, the crisis is at least as catastrophic as that of 1929, but the mistakes made at that time have been avoided thanks to the enthusiastic intervention of central banks and governments. So things cannot be as bad as all that! But we only have to open our eyes to notice the blind march into which our governments have stumbled ever further.

In fact, the incapacity of political leaders to understand this crisis, and consequently to effect solutions to it, is striking, even on the part of the most lucid among them. They act and react in a classic intellectual way, their political responsibility producing a reflex attitude—not

1

to give the citizens too much of a fright, since it is precisely their role, as politicians, to offer solutions and hopes. Even if they claim otherwise, their political horizons go no further than their current electoral term—they have to be seen as reactive and efficient between now and the election. When it comes to a crisis, it might even help them to be perceived as over-reactive!

But when chaotic events occur in succession and seem increasingly to elude the grasp of political leaders, a time will come when the citizens will begin to ask questions, and then turn away from politics, or grow indignant and scandalized before finally arriving at a state of revolt.

Has this point been reached?

The intention in this volume is to anticipate the immediate economic future in the face of a crisis that produces increasingly deleterious effects with each passing day. It thus proceeds from a sense of emergency. My profound conviction is that the world is on the verge of a major economic catastrophe. This conviction is supported by a precise analysis but I should be delighted if it turns out to be wrong.

What is our hypothesis?

Our economic planet is dominated by the ultra-power of a globalized finance whose growing instability is at the root of the most recent crises. For about 15 years, a succession of crises has, each time, required intervention by the International Monetary Fund (IMF), the large central banks and governments.

But when it comes to the present crisis, we encounter a new dreadfully disturbing fact—that governments have been weakened by the massive aid they have had to provide in order to save the financial system from collapse. Therefore, they now have practically no room for budgetary manoeuvre.

Simultaneously, the reforms promised over successive G20 meetings have not fundamentally modified the logics of this global finance, notably the behaviour of its oligopolistic banker core. The result? New speculative booms form, but the gigantic boom in derivatives continues its insane progression. Within these boom formations, that of the Credit Default Swap (CDS[1]) over public borrowing is even more threatening because it places all the indebted states under financial pressure, or, to be precise, under the pressure of globalized finance.

How can one not see that these conditions portend another crisis? And how will governments respond this time?

An analysis of the financial markets, taking Wall Street as the practical and symbolic point of reference, allows a response to these questions. On the one hand, the current financial markets—especially the most important among them, the New York Stock Exchange—have, since the markets were globalized, ceased to fulfil their

---

1 Let us remember that such undertakings allow an assurance against the risk of default (non-payment) by the issuer of a financial security. An allusion is here being made to the obligations set by governments to finance their responses to the financial and economic crisis. The value of these agreements is augmented when the risk of default grows and serves to fix the interest rate against which governments need to borrow on the financial markets.

main function—to finance the economy. Clearly, this is saying something! On the other hand, globalized finance has found in the financial markets the ideal and efficacious vehicle for its 'market activities' or, in other words, its speculative practices.

Finally, and this is not insignificant, financial markets have been and remain the site where the norm of financial profitability initially unfolds and is progressively imposed onto the business world, provoking havoc through its restructuring of the way work is organized and the impact this has on the health of the workers. The 'creation of value for shareholders', apparent over the course of the 1990s, is therefore another fundamental element of anxiety for tomorrow's world.

In order to cope with a world dominated by a financial sphere whose ultra-power comes both from its market practices and the pressure of its shareholder value, do we not need to consider—while bearing in mind the extreme weakness of governments—a world without financial markets in the future, a world without Wall Street?

This project is clearly a political one. This volume is limited to formulating some of its principal lines while trying to develop most of the economic or financial aspects it involves. A world without Wall Street, indeed, but would this promise any amelioration of the current world economic situation? And what is the extent of this proposition?

One of the reasons for this project relates to the negligence of responses brought to bear on the current crisis, and necessarily calls for the formulation of new solutions. In appearance, the diagnosis of the financial crisis has been made thousands of times since its onset, and scenarios (equally numerous) have also been constructed as to a credible solution. What is the result? The vague and persistent feeling that these responses are not really valid, or that they are not at all up to the task of responding to the current planetary dysfunction.

It is therefore necessary to reformulate the paired 'diagnosis–response' relation in other ways. There would be a risk of transforming possibilities into requirements, and therefore of advancing a solution whose a priori credibility would not be clear. This is nevertheless the wager this volume seeks to make by developing the idea that it is possible to conceive, in a future much closer than might be thought, of a world without Wall Street.

Wall Street is actually the keystone, at once symbolic and real, of financial capitalism. Symbolic, because this financial market still signifies, in the public imagination, the world of hyper-powerful finance. And it is also Wall Street which governs the life of the largest companies, notably through their everyday situation analyses (speculator circulation). It is, moreover, a very real keystone— at the end of 2009, this market, along with its European branches, has concentrated close to two fifths of the world speculator capitalization and, during the same year, three fifths of the world exchange of shares.[2]

By conceiving of a world without Wall Street, and especially by acting on it, are we not engaging in a frontal

---

[2] Source: World Federation Exchange (WFE). The data is issued by Nyse Euronext (Europe and the US) and the Nasdaq OMX.

assault upon financial capitalism and its excesses? Certainly, but more than this we are positing the hypothesis that such an assault will be aided by a fresh financial crisis, causing the keystone—along with the entire edifice of the world economy as it is organized today—to topple.

From that point on, a whole universe will have to be rebuilt. But before that happens, we need to explore the paths of reconstruction.

For the present, the initial work, which has to be urgently embarked upon, needs to be symbolic. As well as demonstrating that the time has come to completely change the mental universe, it needs to be understood—for example, by the politicians currently in office—that the market economy must cease its absolute penetration of the financial sphere.

We know from John Maynard Keynes that financial markets are not efficient and that this inefficiency engenders, in a consubstantial way, the speculations of the share market. But, since the 1970s, neoliberal thinking wanted to go a lot further and tried to promote new markets, notably through the liberalization of exchange and interest rates.

This liberalization has proved to be lethal. This volume will show how it has engendered a completely unmeasured extension of markets in derivatives whose role has been fundamental in the current financial crisis.

Consequently, the combat is, first, an ideological one and is concerned, among other things, with the intellectual make-up of economists whose standard thinking has been forged in the light of this very neoliberalism.

In the course of this struggle, a path seems to have opened up by which to think about the method and objectives of a political project that can only be 'alternative'. But, you will ask, is a world without Wall Street really possible and credible? Is this not a new utopia, admittedly attractive but a thousand leagues away from our current universe?

This is partly true. But all we must do is imagine the consequences of the next financial crisis. It will be impossible for governments to respond to it, as they have done to the present crisis, by rescuing banks and budgetarily stimulating their economies. Worse-case scenarios are laid before us. We prefer to anticipate this great shock and propose, before the storm breaks, the great lines of what may be—because it is alternative—an inevitably utopian project. One can only hope to work the idea through in as realistic a way as possible.

The fall of Wall Street will not be mechanical. It will take place with a guiding measure that, when it occurs, will appear obvious and absolutely necessary—the complete prohibition of the derivatives markets, those that have been engendered by the liberalization of the financial sphere.

This volume aims to show that such a prohibition is fundamental if the financial system is to be restabilized and the excessive financialization of human activities arrested. This prohibition must then inevitably be accompanied by a set of rules and measures touching upon the complete panoply of means of financing the economy. They will be measures extending from the global to the most territorialized local context. But how will these decisions be taken? Who will take them? What will be their exact content?

These questions are formidable and demonstrate the extent of the project to be constructed precisely because of the void left in a world without Wall Street. In fact, it could only be a question of a global project whose tenor cannot be limited merely to the economic and financial realm.

Let's look at things more closely.

The credibility of this project will reside, above all, in its mode of elaboration. And this can only be democratic. In fact, the way in which the hegemony of standard economic thinking has progressively imposed itself on political leaders can only leave us aghast.[3] It is clearly necessary to take the opposite direction from that taken by this ideological power.

In the new project, especially in terms of the discipline of economics, intellectual pluralism and tolerance of heterodox ideas should be recommended. Today, this opening up is fundamental so that, through a democratic debate in which citizens and experts are brought face to face, credible solutions to the crisis can emerge, not simply on an economic level but also, more broadly, at the societal level.

---

[3] The terms of a manifesto circulated on 6 September 2010 and subsequently signed by several hundred economists state: 'The economic and financial crisis which shook the world in 2008 has not weakened the domination of the schemas which have oriented economic policies for thirty years.'

What then are the themes and questions that will probably be introduced in the public space and become the object of lively debate? Without here prefiguring definitive solutions, we can at least draw up the list of some of these questions, knowing that they will be dealt with in more detail over the course of this volume.

The elimination of the derivatives markets must entail, in parallel, a whole series of measures concerning the international monetary system. It will be the occasion to engage in an inevitably complicated reflection (but also an essential debate) about the role of money on a world-wide scale with, consequently, an initial question: Should not money be conceived as a common property of humanity?

In the same way, will the disappearance of the present avatar of Wall Street lower the financial pressure currently being exercised over business? Perhaps not. It will consequently be necessary to prolong the struggle against the financialization of business by means of a profound renewal of the question of how businesses results are divided. This question implies in turn—if we really want to eradicate the crazy role of 'shareholder value'—a fundamental reform of property rights in businesses.

In a world without Wall Street, what would be the new role of banks? This question entails reflecting in a profound way on the banking profession and considering how banks could understand the separation, or, more radically, the complete suppression of their renowned 'market activities'.

Another question arises concerning banks: In response to some of their inordinate sizes, would it not make sense for them to be nationalized? This theme imposes itself forcibly by reason of some of their 'systemic' dimensions, or their scale, which is what makes them susceptible (as in the case of Lehman Brothers) to unleashing a world crisis should they fail.

Other connected questions: How would the considerable investments—necessary to respond to the presaged energy crisis—be financed? Could solidarity finance be a way to respond to the environmental and ecological challenges faced by the planet?

One can easily sense that these questions refer to crucial problems of financing that confront the citizens of the entire world who must, very quickly, be directed to think about, to discuss and to find solutions for them. From this perspective, this will remain 'the question of questions' to be resolved: How are we to organize the world democratic powers, as well as those at the other extreme, at the level of the smallest lands, so as to try and bring forth credible and coherent responses?

This last question reveals that the challenges of our times are immense. They are those of a world without Wall Street, whose advent needs to be considered so that the work can begin. Is it not in the end a matter of rediscovering the multiple aspirations both of individuals and of life in society?

PART 1

THE WORLD WITH WALL STREET:
THE IMPASSE

THE ULTRA-POWER OF GLOBAL FINANCE
AND ITS MARKETS

Let us once again consider the question raised in the Introduction: Why has the crisis not ended? It is because the
answers brought to bear on it on the ground are not effective
curative solutions. Therefore it is seriously necessary to raise
the question of a diagnosis, and to dwell upon the profound
causes at its root.

Economic specialists and political leaders responsible for
finding, and setting to work, curative measures have until now
diagnosed two principal causes: the excessive risk taking of
bankers; and the role of tax havens as black holes of international finance. To these are added, as an aggravating factor,
not the deficit but the 'over' leverage of states, the less cynical
of whom recognize that this essentially results from the crisis
itself.

These explanations appear to be largely unsatisfactory and
omit the essential point—the economic and financial planet
has been changed. Since the mid-1990s, the globalization of

monetary and financial markets has reached a decisive stage—worldwide connectivity between all its segments in the trading rooms of the major international banks. At the same time, the complete dematerialization of transactions[1] and the development of 'high-frequency trading'[2] have enforced on the exchanges rules of generalized interconnectivity while allowing the development of what is still an unknown level of world speculative play.

The consequences of these metamorphoses are such that the logics now at work in globalized finance are completely different from those that prevailed no more than about 20 years ago. It is therefore necessary to decipher this new panorama, to understand its origin, to see how its system is constituted and, especially, to show the ways in which its inherent instability lies at the root of the increasingly violent crises we are undergoing.

---

1 Financial markets have now become almost entirely electronic (which is where the term 'de-materialization' comes from) and have assumed the form of data processing between financial institutions. Societies that manage the financial markets, such as Euronext, now consider themselves to be, first of all, service providers of data processing services.

2 This particular form of trading relies on the utilization of computers to manage the orders of purchase and sale of financial securities in an automatic way instead of through individuals communicating face to face or via telephone. This practice allows colossal sums to be gained—through the accumulation of very small margins (of the order of three to four decimals) on very great quantities of flux—in one day. As this practice concerns the great stock exchange indicators, this system influences all the world's stock exchanges in one way or another.

Two great centres of instability are perfectly discernible: the monetary centre; and that of shareholder value. We will see that it was the virulence of the monetary centre—that, from the beginning, accommodated the double liberalization of monetary and financial markets—from which the ultra-power of global finance was progressively deployed. The other centre, eating away at and destabilizing the world economy, is to be found in practices linked to shareholder value. Born from American fiscal laws passed in the 1970s and 80s, the management of pension funds by capitalization is the source of the renowned and feared financial norm of a 15 per cent return on investment.

These two centres are veritable cancers at the core of the world's economy, and therefore for us as world citizens.

AT THE HEART OF THE CRISIS:
THE ULTRA-POWER OF GLOBAL FINANCE

One movement appears fundamental to us—the hypertrophic development of markets of structured products, such as that of derivatives. Its origin is fundamentally due to the insane liberalization of the financial sphere.[3]

One of the essential consequences of this movement is that the power of the major international banks has become phenomenal. This power principally derives its strength from the 'market activities' of these banks which, in turn, stem from their major involvement in the production and circulation of derivatives.

---

3 The analysis of this section is, in part, an updated and synthesized reprise of developments which can be found in François Morin (2006).

These activities, originally meant to cover risks, have now acquired a rather dark aspect and are just as much speculative activities. And this means that speculative forces have become installed in the very heart of globalized finance, and with a considerable destructive power. Worse, the impact of the speculative forces is increased by the effects of leverages linked to debt and by multiple injections of liquidity by the central banks.

The Hypertrophy of Transactions in Derivatives in Inter-bank Exchanges

Very often, the crisis is explained by deregulation, by dysfunction or by unwise incentives. Imprudent actors were guilty of excesses. The financial markets are said to have been poorly controlled or, in some segments, not controlled at all.[4] These factors have certainly played their part: there are risky traders, unsupervised speculative funds, opaque tax havens, myopic rating agencies and even heedless central banks or passive governments.

But if it was simply a question of rashness, deviant behaviour or the weakness of marginal financial organizations, it would be difficult to explain the considerable amounts of losses of value engendered by these financial spasms or escalations. The IMF estimated that, in July 2009, these losses of value amounted to $4,000 million. In the same way, it is difficult to understand how the banks or mortgage funds that

---

4 This vision conforms to the standard economic interpretation, which derives from neoliberal thinking. For a deeper reading of this theoretical sensibility, see Jean Tirole (2008) and Jean-Charles Rochet (2008).

yesterday went bankrupt or are today in turmoil and have had to be rescued from catastrophe by governments are amongst the oldest and often the market flagships. It is therefore really the core of the financial system, in the United States as in Europe, which has been affected.[5]

It is therefore necessary to examine not only the immediate causes of the financial turmoil but also what lies at its very base—the impossible margin carved out for the last 30 years between the financial sphere and the real economy, itself rooted in the processes of the liberalization of the monetary and financial markets.

Just before the sub-prime crisis, the financial sphere had become hypertrophied due to the over-elevated number of security products and the volume of their transactions (see Table 1). In the monetary markets, transactions in the real economy represent only 1.6 per cent of the world's inter-bank exchanges.[6] In terms of flow, the financial sphere is thus almost 50 times greater than the sphere of the real economy. This enormous disequilibrium forms the basis of the derivatives which threaten the entire system. The essential point about inter-bank exchanges thus concerns coverage against variations of price.

---

5 Part of this argument may be found in François Morin and Lionel Jospin (2008).

6 Since the financial liberalization of the 1980s, this ratio has always been less than 3 per cent. On the other hand, at the start of the 70s, it was much higher. According to the figures of the Bank for International Settlements (BIS), calculations prove that for a country such as the United States, the ration was as high as 7.3 per cent—in other words, seven times the current ratio for this country. See *Payment Systems in Eleven Developed Countries* (1980).

	2002	2003	2004	2005	2006	2007	2008
FINANCE ECONOMY							
MARKET OF ORGANIZED CHANGES	23.8	220.6	379.5	545.8	714.3	940.6	1015.0
OTHER ORGANIZED DERIVATES	693.1	874.3	1152.3	1406.9	1080.0	2208.0	1660.0
UNORGANIZED DERIVATES (OTC)	385.7	524.0	545.2	557.8	144.3	147.5	820.4
FINANCIAL OBLIGATIONS (SHARES, BONDS)	38.0	42.7	53.9	64.0	84.1	128.1	132.6
REAL ECONOMY							
GDP	32.3	37.0	41.6	44.8	48.4	54.3	60.1
TOTAL WORLD TRANSACTIONS	1172.9	1698.6	2172.5	2619.3	2799.1	3478.5	3688.1

TABLE 1. THE WORLD ECONOMIC SPHERE

UNIT: the trillion or téra-dollar—a thousand million dollars (T$).

These numbers, which are uncontested, are drawn from the sources of the IMF, the BIS and the World Bank.

For the methodology of this table and its sources, please see www.finance-global.fr and Morin (2006: 253–4).

These are the well-known 'derivatives': 30 per cent to protect themselves against variations in exchange rates; 66 per cent to protect themselves against risks linked, above all, to variations in interest rates but also, to a lesser degree, to fluctuations of speculator circulation, to variations in the price of raw materials and, sometimes, even to credit risks.

There are no security products without a speculative counterpart, since the one who sells such an insurance is making a risky bet against the future. And speculation is fed as much by a bubble forming as it is by fears of the bubble bursting.

The most symbolic example of this speculative management of derivatives is the Abacus affair. The manager of the Paulson & Co hedge (speculative) fund, headed by millionaire John Paulson, collaborated with Goldman Sachs to create a CDO[7] called Abacus. This manager was *counting on the fall in value of this instrument while selling it to investors.* The operation would have cost investors more than a billion dollars. On 15 July 2010, Goldman Sachs admitted to an 'error' in the presentation of its product and agreed to pay a fine of $550 million, the heaviest so far levied in the United States, in exchange for the abandonment of legal action by the American regulator.

In this lack of constraint when it comes to matters of conflict of interests we find one of the destabilizing factors that is *carcinogenic when linked to these practices and products— derivatives can be sold to investors while simultaneously counting on their fall because in reality their toxicity is known*!

---

7 Collateralized Debt Organization (CDO) is a financial product developed around the end of the 1990s to the beginning of 2000. CDOs are representative securities of portfolios of bank credits or financial instruments of a varied nature.

With the crazy extension of these speculative products and funds, the tumour of derivatives is really the cause of the hypertrophy of global finance. Thanks to the bank tool, speculative funds benefit especially from a leverage of gigantic indebtedness which increases their shares.

This is because of the added component of the great responsibility of the banks—it is they who hold or manage the vast majority of speculative funds.

Finally, all of these transactions—located as transactions of the coverage of risks—do not appear in the bank balance sheets. They are only listed in their 'off-balance accounts'.

We can appreciate why, under these conditions, the G20 meetings in London and Pittsburgh wanted to attack the markets in derivatives. But, surprisingly, instead of reducing their influence, indeed of eradicating them entirely, these summits sought only 'to organize them better'! The argument they put forward in their defence was that these markets were operated 'by mutual agreement' and in a 'non-transparent' manner. It is true that the vast majority of transactions in these particular products were not enclosed in a 'clearing-house' which could then allow rules to be fixed relative to the exchanges so as to introduce greater transparency into the transactions.

But, from our perspective, the real question lies elsewhere. The multiplication of derivatives, the excesses of their outstanding debts and the insane volume of their transactions (by mutual agreement) are sources of an unbridled and endlessly growing speculation. In short, the decisions of the G20 were an attempt at controlling the spread of a tumour instead of eradicating it. These measures left the logics at the basis of the formation of coverage products, and therefore of speculative funds, totally unchanged.

Yet, when we analyze the composition of this tumour (essentially, coverage products of exchange and interest rates), all we will have to do is re-examine the double movement of the liberalization of the money markets in order to reduce, at a stroke, the financial sphere. But where did this double movement come from?

We need to remember that the financialization of the world economy is a recent phenomenon whose emergence has been marked by several stages since the Bretton Woods accords of 1944. At the time of this conference, the United States imposed the dollar as the international currency. In order to return to stability and confidence in money, a condition of the Marshall Plan destined to open up an external market to the United States, it was decided to return, provisionally, to the benchmark represented by gold. The return to the gold standard allowed the dollar to affirm its hegemony at the heart of international financial system.

Thanks to the war, the United States accumulated reserves of gold while other countries had hardly any. This meant that, over the following decades, the United States was given the possibility of living on credit while financing its deficit, thanks to the strength of its currency which had become the international reference point.

This American hegemony would, however, encounter an initial limit with the creation of the euro/dollar market in 1958 which allowed the London market to assert itself on the international financial scene.

By 1971, the gold reserves of the United States had progressively dried up. President Richard Nixon decided to abandon the convertability of dollars into gold and, at the same time, to suppress fixed parities between the main currencies.

But the Americans, carried along by habit, would continue to make the dollar the incontestable reserve currency at the international level. In other words, the American currency symbolized a confidence without counterpart other than that accorded to American treasury bonds, since these bonds are bought in dollars.

If the 1971 break was the especially visible sign of a new weakening of the dollar, it was equally the signal of a declining profit ratio in the United States, in itself in great part the result of the considerable American expenditure required to finance the Vietnam War.

With the break with the Bretton Woods accords, and consequently of a dollar whose link with the gold standard had been broken, *an essential stage towards financial globalization was reached. It marked a first great liberalization—that of exchange rates whose fluctuations would then uniquely be determined by the law of supply and demand upon currency markets.*

This fundamental deregulation, encouraged by neoliberal thinking in full flight, swept along in its wake the development of a market in the coverage of risks. It was, in fact, necessary for businesses to insure themselves against incessant variations in the price of different currencies, thus generating very high levels of uncertainty in international commerce.

But, of course, even with these coverages, the exchange risk did not vanish. It was assumed by those who sold coverage products—those who, according to the terminology, are no different from speculators.[8]

---

8 There are several definitions of speculators. From the rather general definition which sees in the speculator a person ready to accept the calculated risks of the market for a capital gain in the short or

The beginning of the 80s was marked by another essential phase. Governments, themselves dependent on the markets for their financing, and influenced by the liberal ideas dominant in the United States and in the United Kingdom under Ronald Reagan and Margaret Thatcher, engaged in an extreme form of deregulation of the financial markets. Reforms of the bank and monetary systems were therefore undertaken in the more developed countries with the creation of vast bond markets in which governments issued loans so as to finance public deficits.

This deregulation was at the root of the *second great liberalization of fundamental rates for finance—those of long-term interest rates.*

Indeed, in renouncing the framing of credit and thereby more or less controlling the various interest rates, long-term interest rates began to vary in tune with supply and demand.

This second deregulation was, like the first, a considerable shock for the real economy. It meant that here, too, it would become necessary to create coverage products so as to insure against variations in these rates.

At the end of the 80s, the markets in derivatives really took off with the inevitable development of speculative practices. For rate risks were still present, as were the speculators to profit from them.

---

medium term, one can develop a more precise definition for someone who intervenes in the financial market—the speculator is someone who is looking to take a risky stand on a financial product and, through that, to make a bet on the future advancement of its value.

Thus 'derivative' products developed powerfully because they were based upon 'underlying' ones like interest rates, stock exchange quotations or even mortgage credits (like the well-known sub-primes in the United States). Worse, these products have enlarged their range of underlying products to include petroleum, raw materials and food. And it is the very nature of these underlying products that has allowed the financial sphere to bite directly into the real economy.

It is necessary, moreover, to underline that, in both cases (exchange rates and interest rates), the liberalization of prices very quickly led to them wanting to protect themselves from their variations!

By the mass of transactions which are linked to them and by the organizations into which they are inserted, these two latter variables of liberalized finance have the capacity to exercise, in their turn, a decisive influence over the variables of the real economy, precisely by reason of the 'global' spectre of their effect.

This represents an essential factor in the 'globalization' of the monetary and financial markets and, consequently, of the growing control effected by the financial sphere over national economies.

In this way, the euro/dollar exchange rate can be known at any moment and at any place on the planet—this is its global spectre. But a brutal variation of its level can destabilize entire countries. In the same way, interest rates formed on the American bondholder market are a guiding rate for the rest of the world's bondholder markets. Here too, one variation in its level can quickly place the public finances of several countries in difficulty.

The course of the globalization of the monetary and financial markets can be charted from the middle of the 1990s. Finance became global. It was then expressed through a series of effects: a considerable development of the derivatives markets; the increase of the dot-com bubble (until it burst at the end of 2000), followed by a deflationary phase of audit balancing; the growth of the real-estate bubble; the crisis of the sub-primes; and, finally, an explosion of public debt. This was the result of several years of financial crises.

But most impressive was undoubtedly the rapidity with which the markets in coverage products developed. Thus, the markets relating to options[9] and futures[10] rose, in terms of outstanding debts, from only 1.7 T\$[11] in 1987[12] to 426.7 T\$ at the end of 2009. This dazzling expansion has not really been halted by the crisis, except for the outstanding debts of the CDS—from 0.9 T\$ in 2001 to 62.1 T\$ in 2007 and 30.4 T\$ in 2009.

It is essential to understand how dangerous these products are because, as has been strongly demonstrated by

---

9 An option is a derivative which gives the right, when it is bought, or the obligation, when it is sold, to buy or to sell an underlying asset at a fixed price in advance during a given time or at a fixed date, whether with a view to speculation or to insurance of insurance.

10 A forward or *future* contract is a firm engagement to buy or sell an agreed quantity of an asset at an agreed price and at an agreed future date. Futures are standardized and quoted products: they concern referent assets for a standard amount and with a fixed expiry date.

11 Or trillions of dollars according to American terminology (a thousand billion dollars).

12 See *BIS Quarterly Review* (November 1996, www.bis.org) and *ISDA Market Survey 2010* (www.isda.org/statistics/pdf/ISDA-Market-Survey-historical-data.pdf) for the most recent figures.

Georges Berlioz, a business lawyer specializing in international finance,[13] their constructions have become uncontrollable. Moreover, the distribution and dispersion of risks of which they boast are illusory. These products are, in fact, completely correlated, and the variation in their prices is not, as they were believed to be, self-compensating. On the contrary, they fluctuate in the same direction.

To sum up, therefore. The virulence of the monetary centre stems, from the beginning, from the double liberalization of the monetary markets—a liberalization of the exchange rates during the 1970s and of the interest rates at the beginning of the 80s. A financial industry in the coverage of risks developed in order to protect the real economy from these two shocks. Companies had to cover themselves against risks linked to variations in the exchange and interest rates. Swelling visibly during the 90s, this industry began to cover risks of all sorts with more and more sophisticated products, all of which were exchangeable on the financial markets.

At the end of the 90s, the banks came up the idea of 'taking out' of their balance statements—by transferring them to societies registered in tax havens—the credits made for individuals or private businesses.

But how should these transfers be paid for? Quite simply, by issuing bondholder securities through these societies (which were not subject to regulation) on the financial markets. By means of this operation, credits on the assets side of

---

13 'Financial and speculative techniques go against the moral principles of justice and equity. They go against reason, in the blindness of the desire to manage commissions . . . The reshaping of capitalism requires a return to conditions of morality and ethics' (Berlioz 2008).

the banks' balance sheets were transformed into financial securities which could then be sold on the markets. With these sales, the banks found themselves in possession of liquidities, and the risks linked to the credit activity were transferred to those who bought the financial securities. In other words, credits were 'securitized' through transactions of deconsolidation of part of the banks' balance sheets.

The securitization of credits was already familiar to the banks. But the novelty consisted in transforming *their real-estate credits, notably for their own account,* into exchangeable financial securities on the market.

By the end of 2006, the real-estate bubble burst in the United States and housing prices collapsed. At the same time, interest rates rose, and the securities linked to the real-estate credits of the most vulnerable American households began to lose their value, since the revenues linked to these securities had melted away.

It was then that these securities became 'toxic'. The phenomenon was all the greater for the fact that these securities were able, in their turn, to enter into the composition of newer securities which were supposedly more 'structured' and complex. Indirectly, these structured securities also became toxic, and it was impossible to determine their exact value. The banks which had invested on their own account in these products then saw their funds progressively lose value.

This piling up of toxic products at the heart of global finance, a veritable carcinogenic centre, could only have developed, as we have seen, thanks to the major international banks and their 'market activities'. As a result, governments were then obliged to transform mountains of private toxic debts into a public super-indebtedness.

The Phenomenal Power of the Major Banks

According to Simon Johnson (of the Sloan School of Management at MIT),[14] the crisis was due, above all, to the concentration of finance in the hands of a few establishments which become so powerful that they were able to impose their views on the regulators. The crisis has increased this concentration even further.

In fact, when we seek to identify the leading forces at work in the post-1990s financial landscape, an obvious fact stands out—the enormous power of the leading international banks.

The banks are the cause of the 'financial innovation' linked to derivatives, and they dominate the market in 'swaps'— contracts that allow an exchange of (naturally risky) variable rates against a fixed rate, called a 'rate swap'. This domination results in the market power that these major banks exercise over the formation of their rates. And it should be borne in mind that these rates are today the reference rates for the whole of the monetary and financial markets. Moreover, at the beginning of the new century, the major banks took control of the majority of societies that managed investment funds on behalf of third parties.

These are the funds which are at the root of the norm of financial profitability which has been affirmed across the entire world over the course of the 90s. We now know the disastrous consequences the presence of these funds has had on the management of companies since they became subject to the growing financialization that favoured the new shareholders.

---

14 See *Le Monde* (27 April 2010) on five non-conformist economists, one of whom was Simon Johnson.

The exchange rates and interest rates that were previously regulated by governments could, after liberalization, be temporarily controlled by the great central banks. Financial globalization has made it possible for the private powers—the great global banks—to manipulate these rates in accordance with their own interests.

These banks today form a particularly powerful international oligopoly: on the one hand by reason of their small number; and on the other due to their considerable financial profits. Relegating the central banks to the second level, confining them to being simple purveyors of the liquidity they need, *this oligopoly is the true operator of the world's monetary and financial markets. It is capable of revitalizing them but also, through excessive risk-taking, of destabilizing them.*

This oligopoly is clearly subject neither to political control nor a fortiori to democratic control. It is only slightly constrained by prudent rules elaborated a posteriori and of limited scope, or else by norms emerging from professional self-regulation, but only after the difficulties or catastrophes have unfortunately taken place.

Clearly, today, it is the biggest banking groups who are at the heart of global finance. Forty-five thousand banks operate in the world.[15] Among them, one can locate the contours of this oligopoly by, for example, glancing at the list of the banks considered 'primary dealers'. These major banks are regularly introduced into the American inter-bank market and alone have the right to respond to certain (generally everyday)

---

[15] According to convergent established sources at the start of the 2000s, from a questionnaire of the BIS, the British Bankers' Association, the Building Societies Association and national sources.

calls for tender from Federal Reserve of the United States (see below). They are consulted by the American Treasury and by the Fedderal Reserve about the state and evolution of the demand for debt security, in order to satisfy in the best possible way the demand for the financing of the American federal state deficit and the implementation of monetary policies.

PRIMARY DEALERS, ON 1 APRIL 2010

- BNP Paribas Securities Group.
- Bank of American Securities LLC
- Barclays Capital Inc.
- Cantor, Fitzgerald & Co.
- Citigroup Global Markets Inc.
- Credit Suisse Securities (United States) LLC
- Daiwa Capital Markets America Inc.
- Deutsche Bank Securities Inc.
- Goldman, Sachs & Co
- HSBC (Securities) (United States) Inc.
- Jefferies & Company, Inc.
- JP Morgan Securities Inc.
- Mizuho Securities USA Inc.
- Morgan Stanley & Co Incorporated
- Nomura Securities International, Inc.
- RBC Capital Markets Corporation
- RBS Securities Inc.
- UBS Securites LLC.

(*Source: the Federal Reserve of the United States*)

Another way of drawing the contours of the bank oligopoly is to refer to the list recently prepared by the Financial Stability Board (FSB), currently working with 30 banks and insurers on systemic risk and the management of international financial crises.[16] These institutions were chosen in terms of what is needed when it comes to cooperation and sharing information but, the Board added, not necessarily on the basis of their systemic importance. Nevertheless, the FSB confirmed that it had identified those financial institutions that were 'active at the global level' and had entrusted their monitoring to one of its colleges of supervision.

But, according to an article in the *Financial Times* (1 and 3 December 2009), the institutions on this list could be considered as 'systemic'—their failure, as with what happened with Lehman brothers, could affect the whole financial sector.

Here is the complete list of the banks and insurers concerned according to the *Financial Times*:

LIST OF BANKS AND INSURERS

North America
Goldman Sachs, JP Morgan Chase, Morgan Stanley, Bank of America-Merrill Lynch, the Royal Bank of Canada

Great Britain
HSBC, Barclays, Royal Bank of Scotland, Standard Chartered

Europe Outside the UK
UBS, Crédit Suisse, Société Générale, BNP Paribas, Santander, BBVA, Unicredit, Banca Intesa, Deutsche Bank, ING

Japan
Mizuho, Sumimoto Mitsui, Nomura, Mitsubishi UFJ Group

Insurers
AXA, Aegon, Allianz, Aviva, Zurich FS, Swiss Re

---

16 According to information given by the Agence France-Presse (AFP) on Monday, 30 September 2009. Let's recall that the FSB was created a year earlier by the G20 in order to respond to the crisis in sub-primes and to avoid a fresh shock. It replaced the Financial Stability Forum (FSF) created in 1999 in order to respond to the crisis in the CTCM speculative fund. This entailed a short but spectacular stock exchange crash in the autumn of 1998.

A final way of identifying the power of this oligopoly is to compare data which contrasts the strength of the largest banks with the financial weakness of governments. Thus, on 31 December 2008, the total balance sheets of the 10 largest global banks, which measured in stocks their capacity to mobilize and allocate resources, was almost equivalent to T\$35.5 or the world public debt (another datum of stock)![17]

The financial crisis has evidently affected these major banks. At the height of the crisis, and according to the estimates of the IMF, two-thirds of the toxic assets were housed in the balance sheets of the banks. But, since the second semester of 2009, the biggest global banks, at least those which have avoided nationalization, very quickly made their voices heard once more. Three subjects illustrate the resurgence of the global bank oligopoly: the will to free itself from the tutelage of governments so as to return to the freedom to fix the remuneration of their senior directors; the concern to limit the extent of stress tests[18] in order not to have to appeal for fresh capital stock; and, finally, the will to exempt themselves from the rules that have been created in order to ensure the best moment for the announcement of their results.

On 9 June 2009, the United States Department of the Treasury authorized 10 of the largest banks in the country to

---

17 For the data about the public world debt, see the website of the *Economist*. Data about bank balance sheets have been drawn from the information in their annual reports. See Appendix 2.

18 Bank stress tests were put in place by the central banks and the authorities in charge of bank supervision. It was a matter of an exercise consisting of the simulation of extreme but plausible financial and economic conditions in order to study the consequences on the banks and to measure their capacity to withstand such situations.

repay $68 billion of public funds—from which they had collectively benefited since the autumn of 2008—in the framework of its plan to stabilize the financial system. One should be under no illusions about the decision of the Obama administration—in reality it very rapidly gave in to the demands of these major banks, desirous as they were of getting rid of the tutelage of the State and, especially, of the limits imposed in terms of the remuneration of the executives.

At the same moment, a debate commenced about stress tests. The American and British banks underwent a series of these tests. If the American banks emerged from them apparently reinforced, we should recall the polemic surrounding the negotiations over their final results. The first tests brought to light a need for an additional capital of $74.6 billion. This number appeared to many observers an under-estimation because it was common knowledge that it had been the subject of heated discussions between the Obama administration and the bankers.

But the economic situation seemed to be tied up with the tests. Indeed, in the United States a second series was envisaged in case the situation worsened. Among the hypotheses maintained at the time of the first tests, destined to gauge the resilience of American banks in the case of a worse economic situation, was a target unemployment rate of 10.3 per cent in 2009. Many experts wondered whether this forecast was too limited in character. The most recent published figures of the American employment situation have shown that their doubts were right.

Thereafter, the institutions tested ceased to have any margin for manoeuvre, except to stimulate a fresh need for stockholder equity. The banks were already reticent about giving up assets at discount prices, to which new losses would have obliged them to agree. The American banks thus engaged in a tussle with the administration and, for the moment, succeeded in slipping through the net of a fresh series of tests.

In Europe, following a political compromise between the principal European regulatory authorities, the initial results of analogous tests became known on 23 July 2010. Seven European banks failed: five in Spain; one in Germany; and one in Greece. Among them, the regulators estimated that the German institution Hypo Real Estate (HRE) was most in need of capital stock and it had to raise €1,245 billion in order to satisfy the minimum requirement.

Several analysts have underlined the 'indulgence' of the tests in relation to the major European banks. Three observations cast doubt on this operation. One, none of the seven institutions that failed was quoted on the stock exchange. So there was no reason for the financial markets to be alarmed.

Two, the tests did not extend to government default. Admittedly, it was difficult for the European authorities to do this, taking into account the new mechanisms of financial stabilization put in place at the beginning of May 2010. Nevertheless, it is clear that today's systemic risk could result from another Greek situation—a European country having difficulties honouring its debts.

Let us finally note that these tests have once again underlined the difference between German institutions and French banks. The French banks resisted the tests more effectively, probably because they are larger and predominantly international, while the German banking system essentially rests on regional banks. Many observers foresee a concentration of the German sector.[19] Indeed, let us not forget that the German banking sector was particularly affected at the height of the crisis, and that several institutions could be the starting point for a systemic instability.

Three, it was at the accountancy level that the bank oligopoly, especially in Europe, obtained its greatest satisfaction. The accountancy authorities in Europe, principally the International Accounting Standards Board (IASB), gave in to pressure from the European public powers. The banks repeatedly indicted the IAS 39 standard, which rests on the notion of 'fair value' in the valuation of financial assets. In other words, its market value. This arrangement effectively forces the banks to recapitalize each time part of their assets loses value by reason of a lowering of the market price. This standard had, however, been imposed by American institutional investors who demanded to be able to follow, over the immediate term, rises in the value of securities. These rules of asset evaluation were significantly relaxed during the crisis; in some countries, they were abandoned altogether on the grounds that the 'market' for several classes of assets had vanished, especially for structured products of debt, the toxicity of which we have already cited. All of this created the unfortunate impression that when the larger banks begin to find the rules unsuitable, it is time for the rules to be changed!

It should be noted that the three subjects raised here had been imposed by the bankers themselves, at the same time

19 We could note moreover that Germany has permanently dragged its feet during this operation. It has long been opposed to the publication of these tests, fearful of being placed on the index. On this subject, see Marie de Verges (*Le Monde*, 27 July 2010).

and on both sides of the Atlantic. Coordination of economic interests is characteristic of any oligopoly.

In spite of the chaotic events, the world banking oligopoly ended up rising like a phoenix from the ashes—its own and those it had unfortunately scattered in its wake.

A Speculation Reinforced by the Injection of Liquid Assets

To grasp the role of speculation in the crisis, it is necessary before all else to distinguish the actors who played key roles in the fall in the value of assets and in the triggering of the crisis in liquidity. The major banks, which had taken excessive risks and accumulated the most significant losses, were central players. But to this should be added the role played by hedge funds.[20] Even if their actions were controversial,[21] let us simply point out that their links with the banks are close and they vie with them in their destabilizing and speculative practices over the financial markets.

Indeed, hedge funds are permanent users of leveraging,[22] notably in the conciliation strategies by which managers seek to amplify the gains linked to price margins. This leverage, which necessitates indebtedness, is provided by their prime

---

[20] Hedge funds are non-quoted investment funds of a speculative inclination. They are contrary to their name, which implies covering, funds whose investment policy is not subject to any restriction, legal or otherwise, and their objective is to obtain positive results regardless of the market situation.

[21] Elements of this controversy were discussed in 'Le crise financière: diagnostic et perspective', a special joint issue of *Revue d'économie financière* and *Risques* (June 2008).

[22] This is the possibility offered by certain products or financial practices to multiply the gains or losses for the same initial investment. This consists, for example, in buying a security while possessing only

brokers[23] via credit lines or loans of securities. These are the major international banks which assure the function of prime brokerage, the very same ones that have been caught in the turmoil of the crisis of sub-prime derivatives. At the height of the crisis, these banks wanted to obtain liquid assets at any price in order to clean up their balance sheets. Their activity of prime brokerage was then strongly reduced, leading to strained relations with hedge funds as an immediate conse-quence. The latter were among their best clients due to the importance of paid assigned commissions—as high as 25 per cent of the revenues of their investment bank.[24] This situation must have hastened the collapse of several hedge funds and, in their wake, of several banks.[25]

As Michel Aglietta has quite correctly pointed out, hedge funds act as a 'mimetic pack' in a period of stress and this is precisely what helped precipitate the crisis.[26] They were there-fore the generators of systemic risk. In order to be able to save

---

a part of the sum required, then in selling it at a higher quotation. The leveraging is then the relation between the surplus thereby real-ized and the starting price. Or imagine the situation on the foreign exchange market (Forex): with $1,000 and a leveraging of 100, you can invest $100,000. In the market, the effects of the leverage pro-posed will generally be from 100 to 500.

23 In practice, the prime brokers are the banks that allow hedge funds to organize their activities.

24 See Alain Dubois and Jean-Pierre Mustier (2007).

25 In the United States alone, four major banks vanished: Bear Stearns, Lehman Brothers, the Countrywide and Washington Mutual funds. As well as more than 250 small and medium-sized banks.

26 Professor of economics at Paris-X Nanterre and advisor at the Centre d'Etudes Prospectives et d'Informations Internationales. See Michel Aglietta, Sabrina Khanniche and Sandra Rigot (2010).

the individually untenable positions they were no longer able to finance, they were constrained massively to sell securities so as to recoup liquidity, causing the stock exchanges to fall. In addition, their conciliation strategies aim to profit from market anomalies. Therefore, if some hedge funds consider that the situation will get worse, they may openly continue to sell,[27] reinforcing the spiral which leads to a systemic crisis.

It is finally necessary to recall the key role played by the central banks in the monetary markets. By lowering their rate directives to the minimum points, the American Federal Reserve proposed exclusive rates of between 0 and 0.25 per cent from December 2008 and the Central European Bank a rate of 1 per cent from 7 May 2009. What was the consequence? Fuel was added to the fire! Enormous injections of liquidity—first into the banks and then to the financial markets which were already gorged on liquidity.

The result was that liquidity increased from 17 per cent per year in 2002 to 20 per cent (see Artus and Virard 2007).[28] This excess was the cause, before the crisis, of a massive use of credit to boost certain economies. For example, this boost

---

27 This situation was, for example, encountered from December 2009 with Greek bonds. By openly selling Greek government bonds, the hedge funds precipitated the flight of spreads (the variations of interest rates against those in Germany).

28 This volume demonstrates how an excess of liquidity nourished speculations and booms, and confirms the perversity and the danger of the monetary mechanisms at work before us. What follows in this section is inspired in part by these authors. In part only, because they omitted to speak about how the excess of liquid assets injected by the central banks had its source in reality—in the very functioning of the financial markets, especially in the behaviour of the banks.

provoked the enormous external deficit of the United States. But it was a deficit that could be financed up to the present by the accumulation of exchange reserves in dollars in Asia and in the oil-producing countries. So long as the dollar remains the international reserve currency, this accumulation will continue. But for how long?

It is the monstrous increase of world liquid assets, created by the central banks, that has thus entailed the excess of indebtedness and the booms in the asset price. The crisis of the sub-primes has not stopped the injection of liquid assets, since the central banks have been forced to inject more in order to avoid the collapse of the international banking system. The bubbles created from this excess nourish one another—the drying up of real-estate credits has directed liquidities towards other assets, in particular raw materials and food products.

There are therefore compelling reasons to think that what has been done to ward off the current crisis will drag the world economy towards other, still more devastating, crises. They aggravate one of the principal dangers threatening it—an excess of money.

Between 1988 and 2008, the world liquid assets went from 8 to 19 per cent of the planet's GDP. Briefly interrupted by the crisis, this elevation has again increased over the past year. It is fed by two springs: the accumulation of the currency reserves of the emergent countries;[29] and the monetary measures taken

---

[29] The accumulation of reserves is the source of monetary creation to the extent that the central bank finds itself the holder and uses these reserves to buy, for example, financial securities. This purchase then spreads fresh liquidities.

by the central banks of the rich countries. In order to loosen the stranglehold of credit, these banks have enriched their traditional arsenal (lowering rates in the short term) while having recourse to so-called unconventional means: by themselves directly re-purchasing sovereign debt securities. These purchases contribute towards the flooding of the world economy with still more liquid assets.

What might the result of this be? New booms in the price of assets—shares, real estate, raw materials—and a predictable havoc provoked by their collapse.

The merit of the Artus and Virard volume is that it exposes the vicious circles preventing the system from returning to equilibrium. So everyone today recognizes that obstinately maintaining long-term interest rates below the growth rates of the economy (the great instigator of this policy was Alan Greenspan, former president of the Federal Reserve) results in a 'pathological' indebtedness which in turn nourishes the speculative boom.

This means that the central banks are today confronted with a dilemma—their anti-speculation weapon should be a stiffening of monetary policies, but they refrain from doing so for fear of disrupting the recovery. Then (as we have noticed recently and as happened during earlier crises), the bubbles begin to reappear even before the growth. In addition to the risks they create, they hinder the 'real' economy by once again making liquid assets vulnerable to speculation.

Another self-maintained mechanism is that the external American deficit increases the exchange reserves of the emergent countries. These are converted by the countries with surpluses (principally China) into American bonds, which in turn causes a lowering of interest rates in the United States. This long-term lowering of interest rates stimulates demand and increases the external American deficit. The equilibrium thus created is a ceaselessly deepening 'equilibrium of disequilibrium', a kind of equilibrium of terror between the Chinese and the Americans. For how long?

THE FOUNDATION OF THE CRISIS:
THE IMPOSSIBLE DEMANDS OF SHAREHOLDER VALUE

Alongside the wound which speculation forms round derivatives, the other great infectious centre, which eats away at the world economy and destabilizes it, resides in connected practices through 'the creation of value for shareholders'. These new practices emerged when the large institutional investors[30] changed their behaviour following the adoption of several fiscal arrangements made in the United States (the Erika Law and Amendment 401k).[31] The management of pension funds by these large investors changed entirely during the 1980s, passing from a system of 'Defined Benefits', or DB funds, to a system of 'Defined Contribution', or DC funds.

---

30 How institutional investors are described is variable: in the work of the Committee on the Global Financial System (CGFS), they may indiscriminately be called institutional managers or, better still, collective managers. Among them the Committee distinguishes in particular the managers of 'house' funds, and managers of external funds who act on behalf of third parties. About these denominations, see Michael Cardona and Ingo Fender (2003).

31 The funds called 401k are so named in reference to the article of the tax code anticipating fiscal advantages for those who put money into it.

FRANÇOIS MORIN

In the system of DB funds, the future pensioner knew beforehand the amount of pension he or she would receive, because it was directly related to the contribution he or she made during his career. The manager of the funds, who received the contributions, therefore had to guarantee— through investments made on the stock exchange—the amount of pension expected. Consequently, he had to manage the investments in question like 'a good head of the family' because, in the end, he was the one who had to assume the risk connected to the stock exchange transactions.

In contrast, in the DC system, the risk linked to stock exchange investments is not assumed by the manager of the funds but by the future pensioner. In this new system, the future pensioner knows how much his contributions will be and he may know those made by his employer but, unlike in the DB system, he does not know beforehand the fraction of the revenues to be assigned to him when he retires. This new system, a priori unfavourable to employees, was nevertheless put in place thanks to substantial fiscal incentives. But there was at least one further, and equally essential, reason—the prospect of considerably greater yields in the new system. This is what we will now examine.

In the United States, the amounts assigned to the future pensioners of a scheme are centralized in a 'trust' which does not have the power to manage the sums so collected. Against this, it is able to choose the different managers who have the right to offer their products to contributors. *The choice of these managers is carried out on the basis of the criterion of financial performance*. It follows that what has been created by these reforms is *a competitive market in the management of products of long-term savings*.

Then, because of the competition engaged in by the principal managers so as to reap the retirement savings, the management of DC-type funds became a lot more aggressive as it sought the highest possible financial profit on its investments.

This new form of management also had consequences for the composition of investment portfolios which evolved towards a dominant 'action' in order to benefit from the market premium.[32] This structural given impelled funds to seek to couple the highest possible yield with risk, and meant that their investment policy became more aggressive than that of management as 'a good head of the family'. Consisting of a more targeted approach, it sought to outperform the stock exchange indicators.

From the middle of the 90s, not only can the trend we have previously evoked of a globalization of monetary and financial markets be observed, but so too can that of a radical change in the management of pension funds. Indeed, it is also from that moment that the total DC-type funds in the United States acquired greater volume than the DB-type.

How did this new way of managing funds translate into the balance sheets of institutional investors? This consideration brought to light a double mechanism for the postponement of risks: for liabilities, the sums collected by way of pension savings comprise no risk, since this risk is transferred, as we have seen, to future pensions; for the assets, the investment securities are not risked either, as we shall now show.

---

32 Historically, the existence of the market premium allowed shares to offer a higher yield than the ensemble of other forms of financial investment, even if the real rate that emerged over 15 years only allowed a real yield on average of 6 per cent.

Indeed, these new financial 'intermediaries', those managing DC-type funds, became the true masters of the financial evaluation of the capital sums invested in the stock exchange. They would, in fact, progressively establish their power over the business world by requiring the introduction of new standards in the very functioning of businesses quoted on the stock exchange. The principle of these norms was the well-known 'creation of shareholder value'. We see in this the clearly visible interest of these financial investors who became, as time passed, the principal investors in quoted businesses.

After being observed in the United States and in England, the reversal of logic in the management of pension funds instigated the hegemony of this 'shareholder value' over the financial markets of the entire world.

Now is the time to explain what lies behind this notion, which is essentially a matter of extracting value at the heart of companies and which goes well beyond any profit that might be considered normal.[33] The production of this 'supervalue' was prescribed by the new shareholders—those who managed DC-type funds. Due to their numbers and the impact of their contributions on the capital of quoted companies, these investors were in a position to impose on company management a certain number of norms in matters of business governance, the most important of which was that of financial profitability fixed at 15 per cent. The amount of this ratio was imposed very quickly but without any real foundation being assigned to it. This norm dominated all of the others, and it was conceived by the investors as a pledge of the efficacy of their investments.

---

[33] A profit is said to be 'normal' when it results from a maximization under constraints.

The practices linked to shareholder value affect all the companies that are quoted across the world's financial markets. But, post-2000, the large investors have become increasingly interested in non-quoted businesses. There, as the risk appears to be greater, the requirement of profitability passes to a distinctly higher level—to almost 25 per cent!

Although until 2007 the world economy grew at an average annual rate of 4 per cent, such a rate appeared completely excessive because it preyed on the activity and results of the business. The extension of this terrifying logic to an immense number of businesses was, to use a medical analogy, comparable to a proliferation of carcinogenic metastasis on our economic and social fabrics.

The financial norm implies that the managers of funds, as shareholders, become ultra-demanding when, for example, they place the resources entrusted to them in companies quoted on the stock exchange. Behind the formulae of 'shareholder value', of the 'creation of value for shareholders' or even of 'stockholder sovereignty', there should therefore be seen the increasing hold of institutional investors on business management and the financialization of this form of management.

The 'new governance' of companies has completely changed the face of businesses, their management and organization. Demands for a financial yield fixed a priori effectively imply a transfer of massive risk onto the management of the business[34] which then sees itself constrained to an obligation

---

34 With this sort of behaviour, institutional investors transformed the vision of the business by turning it into a pure financial patrimony preoccupied with valorizing its assets. We are still far removed from a conception of business in which the 'social interest' is an

for results—to reach, according to the particular case, the 15 or even 25 per cent norm of financial profit. Before the establishment of this new framework, businesses had only an obligation of means—to maximize profit, or in other words to obtain the best possible results after taking into account the constraints encountered. These were notably 'social constraints' which, for example, left a margin to negotiate social compromises.

The introduction of a financial norm, due and known a priori, changed everything and overturned the management of businesses.[35] The consequences this obligation for results has had on the governance and management of companies are multiple.[36]

One, the mechanism of the stock options was a powerful means to encourage senior management to create value for shareholders. How? By giving the directors the right to buy shares in the business at a price (called the 'strike') fixed in advance, with a 'below par' rating in relation to its circulation

essential value and whose aim is the creation of wealth thanks to collaboration between stakeholders. See Dominque Plihon (2003: 116).

35 There was another reason impelling the existence of this norm. As Geoffroy Raduriau explains, this norm 'is deeply linked with the self-referential character of the evaluation. In the markets, investors limit uncertainty by founding their beliefs on the beliefs and strategies of other participants. They seek to know what the others are thinking, will think or are going to do at any given moment. These co-movements are possible in a systemic context, in which a rationality of a self-referential type is dominant, leading to the existence of networks of value' (2010: 74).

36 This new framework, which will be described later, has been examined in a report made to the French government (see Morin 1998).

on the stock exchange.[37] The directors were then encouraged to do everything to augment the stock market circulation of the business, the source of the supplementary valuation of the capital held by the shareholders.

The directors then put to work every option favourable to the creation of this value for the shareholders (but also for themselves!). This thereby satisfied the obligation for results imposed by the norm of financial profitability.[38]

Two, there was the introduction, in management methods, of the criteria of the Economic Value Added (EVA). This has historically constituted the most visible element of the change especially in seeking to impose a financial policy focused on the raising of rates of indebtedness of the business. The EVA measured the effect on financial profitability of a more or less important recourse to indebtedness, from a given

---

[37] This system in general consists of a pre-determined delay (of two to five years). If the director decides to raise an option, he buys the shares at the strike. He will then realize a gain when he sells them again. There is no risk of loss because if the circulation of the shares is lower than the strike, the employee does not exercise his option.

[38] It is only in a relatively recent way that economic theory has acknowledged this new power of shareholders through the normative theory of agency, whose origin goes back to Michael Jensen. This theory was then used for works on the governance of companies in relation with shareholder sovereignty, notably in the works of Andrei Shleifer and Robert Vishny (1997). In this theoretical approach, the directors are the 'agents' of their 'principals', the shareholders. It is then enough to align the interests of the directors with those of the shareholders so that they act in the same direction, that of shareholder value. For a thorough investigation, see Henry Hansmann and Reinier Kraakman (2002).

economic profitability. This technique could thereby be the source for the creation of a supplementary value for the shareholders by playing only on the structure of financings of the business.

Three, the obligation for results can be attained by the technique of so-called capital 'accretion'—reducing the number of shares of a company and thereby allowing, at the end of the exercise and for the same amount of profit, higher dividends to be assigned to the shareholders. How to obtain this accretion? First of all, the company itself can buy back its shares on the stock exchange and then suppress them from the balance sheets, since the same shares are to be found simultaneously as liabilities and as assets.

This practice has only one aim: to raise the dividends assigned to the shareholders effectively by drawing upon businesses' cash reserves, since this cash reserve has served to buy the shares which later on will be concealed.

Four, searching in this way for a financial profitability that is fixed a priori touches upon the strategic decisions bearing on the furthest extent of the activities of the business. There is thus a particularly onerous tendency to reduce the number of its domains of activity. This reduction is, by its nature, entirely linked to the quest for financial performance and the elimination of cross subsidies between activities of the same group.[39] Indeed, for the investors, who enjoy unequal access to information in comparison with what is available to

---

39 Cross subsidies between branches of the same group do not allow external observers to locate the beneficiary activities of those running at a loss. Consequently, for financial investors, these subsidies are an obscure factor and a matter of mistrust.

the directors, the financial transparency of a business goes hand in hand with a reduction in the number of its activities. It allows investors to control the financing of each activity contingent on their own sectorial interests.

The expression of this constraint is translated concretely for businesses by transactions of transfer or division. These techniques in effect allow, in distinct and specialized judicial structures, the different activities of companies to be isolated and assessed; they facilitate the identification of those activities contributing value and those that today consume it but are potentially profitable. This increasing transparency gives institutional investors an essential power of a macrofinancial nature on the planetary level—that of managing the circulation of the flow of liquid assets and the economic values between the different businesses and activities of the entire world.

Thus, the total transfer of the overvalue, created by the obligation for results, to the shareholders (or investors) dispossesses directors of the power of assigning surplus liquidities which until then belonged to them. From that point on, the right to make decisions about the re-assignment of the fruits of business activity are transferred from the business to the shareholders.

Institutional investors can then use the value so released to finance, with capital stocks, businesses which will probably initially make a loss but whose profit potential is higher. The allocation of resources generated by the activity of the business thereby bypasses management teams to move instead through market mechanisms. *The financial market becomes the principal mode of the financial re-allocation of capital, and the institutional investors become its central actors.*

Finally, the obligation for results to which the company is subject weighs on its investment policy. The company must absolutely improve its economic performance. Other than the classical practices which allow the augmentation of gains through productivity, the company becomes committed to new paths which consist, mostly, of transferring all or part of the risk linked to investments to its partners. Let us enumerate the main practices here: the development of the networks of companies, notably for sub-contracting; the multiplication of partnerships; and the externalization of tasks judged not to be critical.

What conclusions can be drawn from these new management orientations linked to the obligation for results to which businesses are from that moment subject? We will bear in mind that the global tendency towards the elevation of financial yields follows directly from the heightened competition of fund managers in the collection of resources linked to retirement savings. The other tendency, relative to the equalization of these same yields (the financial norm), follows from the refusal of institutional investors to assume the reality of the risks linked to their investment activity by transferring these risks to other actors, in particular salaried savers and businesses. One result of these new behaviours is the disappearance today, on speculator markets, of the increasing relation between yield and risk. In some countries, the risk is systematically too high in relation to the average yield observed. In others (notably those of the OECD, the Organisation for Economic Cooperation and Development), the apparent risk is too weak to justify the average yields.

The result of these distortions is speculative management on an international scale, which institutionally instals systemic risk at the heart of the international financial markets. The risk is, in fact, installed 'institutionally', because the vehicles of its diffusion are powerful financial investors, essentially managers of third-party accounts who transfer the risk to other actors.

The risk then assumes a 'systemic' character because the behaviour of these large investors is almost always mimetic. Indeed, when the risk is established and materializes as a crisis, these actors act in the same way and contribute not to reducing it but, on the contrary, to accentuating it, step by step, through a contagion, often over an extremely short period.

The large groups within the model of continental capitalism—even the Anglo-Saxon model in which the banks played the role of primary intermediary through the credits they accorded to them—had to face up to a veritable upheaval. In the space of a few years, the dissolution of these models for the benefit of 'finance market' capitalism has truly modified the nature of these capitalisms.

An ultra-powerful global finance has developed in less than 20 years during which time the major banks have shaped an oligopolistic core whose activities are highly speculative. In the same way, institutional investors, whose capitalistic management usually stems from these same banks, exercise a form of financial pressure over the business world that is nothing short of extravagant.

What means are available to fight against these new logics, laden with serious dysfunctions? No doubt there are no miracle solutions. Should, for example, the United States agree to return to fiscal laws favourable to the development of DC-type funds? In all likelihood, the lobby of large investors will oppose this with all its strength, because the management of risk linked to their investments will come back like a boomerang.

Other avenues merit being explored and will be considered in the second part of this work. For now let us return to the outrageous hold exercised by the financial markets over the business world. And this impels us seriously to envisage the abolition of the link with the large finance markets, like Wall Street, because of the considerable shockwave that the new financial practices have brought upon the real economy.

THE SHOCK WAVE ON WORK, THE ENVIRONMENT
AND POLITICAL ACTION

From a crisis in regulation, to deregulation in crisis, the development of the history of the accumulation of capital always responds to the pressure of profit rates—'when there is a rise we deregulate; when there is a fall we regulate'.[1] From this point of view the crisis we are experiencing today is thus not new. We are confronted with a logic running throughout the economic history of the past two centuries.

What is striking about the current sequence is the enormity of the shock, the rapidity of its extension and the depth of its dysfunction. But it is especially the feeling that the economic and financial system is probably, and for the first time, coming up against its own limits.

The ultra-power of the financial sphere is to be found at the heart of global deregulation, and the speculative activity of its oligopolistic banking core is at its centre. To this is added

1 See François Houtart (2008). Houtart was invited to present his views on the financial crisis to the General Assembly of the UN. Several of his reflections have enriched this chapter.

shareholder value which, borne by financial investors, feeds on hyper-profits.

We should not then be surprised at the devastating effects of the crisis and the logics which underlie it not only at the economic and financial level, and not only at a social and political level. The ultra-power of the financial sphere in the course of the past few decades has so expanded that it outstrips all the facts of the problem.

The crisis through which we are living is a true crisis of civilization, characterized also by the risk of depletion of the planet and an extinction of the living, and thus entailing a veritable crisis of meaning. Consequently, one cannot foretell when exactly it will occur nor what action we can undertake to prevent or combat it.

What is fundamentally new is the convergence between the logics of deregulation to which the world economy has today been introduced. This convergence has been felt in the strength of the shock wave whose full force has struck three intrinsically connected realms. One, the world of work, in which unacceptable inequalities have been carved out. Two, our planet, which is now experiencing irreversible shocks while being on the verge of a major energy crisis. And three, political action, which, outstripped by the extent of these problems and incapable of resolving them, has been pulverized by 40 years of neoliberal practices and thinking.

This shock wave radiates from the playground of financial markets. The latter, in the image of Wall Street, no longer fulfil their primordial function of financing businesses and have become, rather, places in which the speculative forces of globalized finance are concentrated.

The generalization of practices linked to shareholder value entails considerable effects on work relations, the job market and the way work is organized. The consequences of this upheaval, practices of flexibility, outsourcing, offshoring and relocating, have multiplied over the past 20 years.

These new forms of business management entailed, above all, the deformation of added value to the detriment of wage earners during the 1980s and 90s. They lie at the source of the glaring inequalities of incomes we observe today in all the developed countries. Their consequences—in terms not only of precariousness and poverty but also of stress and health—are more and more unacceptable.

The Transfer of Risk on to Wage Earners

In the midst of business, especially of the largest companies, the seeking of 'super' profits linked to the 'creation of value for shareholders' provoked a series of very serious consequences for the world of wage earners. The flexibility of the job market, which assumes that the work force will quickly adapt, destabilizes the formation of skills which, on the contrary, requires a long time if such skills are to be effectively deployed.

The flexibility of the salaried mass, in making employment a variable of adjustment, multiplies the implementation of layoffs, even when companies show profits! This is expressed effectively by the formula of 'redundancy' by which, in order to raise the share price of a company and thereby impart surplus value for shareholders, the directors no longer hesitate to lay off their workers.

The flexibility of the organization of work, founded solely on the search for results and a new mode of business governance, has produced an alarming development of psycho-social risks and a degradation of working conditions, sources of stress, illnesses and psychic sufferings. Pushed to an extreme, these practices result in suicides among employees and discomfort for directors and executives. This is not simply the monopoly of the most developed countries. For example, in the Foxcom society in China, 11 suicides were reported in just the first six months of 2010.

These new orientations appear as a series of processes through which risks are transferred onto salaried workers.[2] It is not enough to make a profit. It is necessary, no matter what consequences will follow for the workers, to attain the result norms expected by the new shareholders.

Despite this, shareholders no longer assume the risks linked to the activity of the business. This risk is carried forward on to the business itself—on to its directors on the one hand and, more profoundly, on to the world of the wage earners on the other, producing a set of internal and external upheavals. First of all, the individualization of the relation they have towards work to the detriment of collective relations; and second, the formation of a network company and its outsourcing (subcontracting, relocating).

---

2 See Patrick Artus and Michèle Denonneuil, for whom risk is now borne by work and no longer by capital. In this scenario, the structure of risk premiums should (in theory) be completely reviewed, in particular the yield of shares which should be just a little higher than that of bonds; and salaries should be, on average, greater to compensate the cyclical character of the salaried mass (1999: 90).

In the realm of management, the individualization is done in the name of 'autonomy' and 'responsabilization'.[3] In reality, these practices engender the intensification of work and self-exploitation. Work time is more and more shattered and more and more difficult to measure. Wage earners are controlled less by the hierarchy than by the definition of targets, by the ratings of client satisfaction and by the armoury of quantitative and qualitative indicators introduced by information technologies. It is the direct consequence of the putting into practice of 'management by targets' utilized with the object of optimizing costs, especially of manpower.

In the end, the new forms of the organization of work have not eliminated overworking. They have, rather, increased it through the physical and psychological burden linked to intensification, to permanent changes, to stress and insecurity in employment.

As for the shape of the network company, it is established to rethink work. This, too, is a question of mastering and measuring costs (particularly salary costs), by placing firms of the same group in competition, on an international scale, by grading them and, if necessary, by sanctioning them (by lowering salaries or by laying off staff). Management teams always react with the same obsessive logic—they privilege flexibility in all of its forms, those of the work force, the teams, the hours, while assigning targets in terms of quality and client satisfaction.

This obsession with flexibility, contrary to its promised objective, often induces a long-term lowering of a company's efficiency. The reactivity of an organization in step with the

---

3 See Patricia Vendramin (2010).

immediate economic conjuncture, as measured by the quarterly results by 'stockholder mood', is not at all a guarantee of financial health.

The Deformation of Added Value

Some people would have us believe that the way the rewards of work and capital are shared have presented a great stability for more than 40 years at the heart of the OECD.[4] The debate about a more balanced sharing of added value and the fruits of growth did not really get off the ground. There was admittedly a strong deformation of the share in added value in work's favour around 1980 in practically all countries of the OECD, but this was an exception due to particular historical conditions (high inflation), and it could not consequently constitute a reference point. According to the supporters of this vision, it would be artificial to modify the way added value is allotted in work's favour.

Other economists contend that the declining role of salaries in added value no longer seems to arise from a conjectural phenomenon but, rather, from a fundamental shift.[5]

---

4 See the Institut national de la statistique et des études économiques (INSEE) reports by Jean-Philippe Cotis to the president of the French Republic and Conseil d'analyse économique (CAE) reports of Gilbert Cette, Jacques Delpa and Arnaud Sylvain to the prime minister. They note that this global stability has been accompanied, since the second half of the 1990s, by a strong augmentation of disparities at the heart of the salaried share of the added value. It is linked, on the one hand, to a strong progression of the highest salary earners and, on the other, to the relative lowering of remuneration of the vast majority of wage earners, the 'middle class'—almost 80 per cent of the wage earners whose salary is above the first decile and below the ninth decile.

Two effects conjoin to cause an augmentation in profits and a reduction in salaries. On the one hand, the movement of outsourcing, whether it is a solution or a threat. On the other, the loss of negotiating power by wage earners at the heart of developed countries.

This movement in the deformation of the division of added value is cumulative, because it weighs on growth. Instead of encouraging businesses to put capacity-building investments to work, it reinforces productivity gains.

In order to see clearly into the heart of this debate, one can easily refer to the latest international data that INSEE has published.[6] The study was concerned with the years 1970 to 2007 and retraced the share of salaries in added value for the countries of the OECD. A look at the data referring to five countries—the United States, Japan, the United Kingdom, Germany and France—prompts several observations:

• the lowest level on the part of wage earners in added value was, for each of these five countries, in 2007;

• the highest level of this share of wage earners was situated in every country between 1970 (in the United States) and 1981 (France);

• the deformation of the share of added value, to the prejudice of wage earners, is a tendency which was observed, consequently, over the entire period of 1970–2007 (see Appendix 1);

5 See Patrick Artus and Marie Paule Virard (2005).

6 'Rapport sur le partage de la valeur ajoutée, le division des profits et les écarts de rémunération en France', INSEE (June 2009). See, especially, TABLE 1.9. Available at: www.insee.fr/fr/publications-et-services/default.asp?page=dossiers_web/partage_VA/partage_VA.htm

- the fall in the share of wage earners stretches, between the highest point of this period to the lowest, from 6.2 per cent for the United States to 17.4 per cent for Japan (UK 8.3 per cent, Germany 9.2 per cent, France 11.3 per cent);

- finally, if we take an average of the preceding data, the fall in the wage earners' share in the five countries reaches 10.5 per cent over the period in consideration.

These tendencies are sufficiently oppressive for the conclusion to emerge clearly here—the way in which revenues were shared has been overturned since the 1970s, precisely from the beginning of the liberalization of the financial sphere. Profits began to grow relatively quicker than wages by reason of the growth in speculative activities linked to the new functioning of the monetary and financial markets.

From the 1990s, the impossible demands of shareholder value have come to be added, augmenting, once more, the share of dividends in added value. The result, as we can guess, is an unprecedented growth of inequalities at the very heart of the most developed countries. This already unacceptable reality becomes unsustainable when we see the consequences faced by the rest of the world.

The Growth of Inequalities of Incomes and Patrimonies

The Capgemini and Merrill Lynch report on world wealth and its distribution was published in June 2008 and showed that 95,000 people have at their disposal a patrimony of 13.1 T$—more than a quarter of the whole wealth produced in the world in 2006.

We are therefore in the presence of a privileged caste which appropriates a major part of the resources of 6.7 billion people. This caste constitutes a 'new aristocracy', which is little concerned with a more equitable distribution of wealth. At the other end of the scale, in the countries of the south, hundreds of millions of men and women live at the limit of the minimum of subsistence.[7] In the northern countries, poverty sets in and work becomes increasingly precarious. Today's crisis is therefore the tell-tale sign of a major disequilibrium bringing into question the very foundations of our economic system.

When 1.4 billion humans live on the threshold of poverty[8] (and this number is increasing); when tens of thousands of people die of hunger every day; when ethnic groups, ways of life and cultures disappear, placing the patrimony of humanity at risk; when the climate deteriorates; when one has to wonder whether it is still worth living in New Orleans, in the Sahel, in the Pacific Islands, in Central Asia or along the ocean, the crisis is not only financial but also social.[9]

The consequences of the latter point are therefore experienced well beyond the frontiers of its origin—unemployment, the high cost of living, the exclusion of the poorest, the vulnerability of the middle classes and lengthening lists of victims over time.

---

[7] The minimum of subsistence reflects the consumption of a basket of goods and services judged indispensable to attain a basic level of life.

[8] In 2008, the World Bank fixed the threshold of international poverty at $1.25 per day.

[9] See Houtart (2008).

Finally, why would private funds in search of financial profitability respond to the fundamental needs of those who have only a reduced or non-existent purchasing power? Incapable of producing added value and having only a weak capacity for consumption, they are no more than a useless crowd, at best susceptible to becoming the object of welfare policy. Once again, it could be said that the logic of accumulation has prevailed over the needs of human beings. But an aggravating fact for the ultra-power of a now-globalized finance is that it is still necessary to make more, and to do so more quickly.

A SECOND EFFECT:

THE ECOLOGICAL AND ENVIRONMENTAL DISASTER

Under pressure from the financial sphere, multinational companies know that, to be able to show the profitability expected of them, they need to act in a space that is free from all constraint. The path to super-profit for them necessarily passes through 'free trade' in all its forms. In clear terms, free trade for companies is the capacity to implant themselves anywhere on the planet, to produce what they want, at times in the worst possible conditions, and to sell this product without constraint.

In this global race towards financial profitability, the only environmentally tolerated solutions must be compatible with the system of free trade—for example, in the image of the scandalous 'market' in emissions trading. There is no appeal against the outcome. During the past 10 years, greenhouse-gas emissions have increased by at least 25 per cent. If the social indicators are already at red, the ecological indicators are unfortunately also going along the same route.

Since the 1970s, free trade has thus entailed the over-exploitation of natural resources, multiplying the pollution-causing transportation of goods as well as encouraging the means of personal travel, with no consideration of climatic and social consequences. The use of petrol derivatives such as fertilizers and pesticides has become widespread in productivist agriculture. The way of life of the upper and middle social classes has been constructed on energy squandering.

The solutions that have been attempted as a response to the energy challenge do not escape the new logic of company financialization—maintaining financial profitability requires ignoring such negative externalities as the environmental effects generated by production. The cost of these externalities has to be supported by collectivities or individuals. For example, the monoculture of biofuels entails ecological consequences which the companies do not take into account—the destruction of biodiversity and of the soil, of underground and of surface water.[10] At the social level it results in the expulsion of millions of small peasants who go on to populate shanty towns and thus increase migratory pressures.

A mode of financialized growth requires that we go ever more quickly and entails most often an ill-considered use of

---

10 The degradation of water quality can result in the deterioration of ecosystems and even their collapse. An excessive load of nutriments into fresh water and coastal ecosystems can lead to the proliferation of algae and a deprivation of oxygen and ultimately make animal life practically impossible. The ecological disaster of the Aral Sea is an example of this catastrophic condition. The diversion of the waters of a river can also be the source of acute political tensions. It is the case at present for the waters of the Jordan, the Euphrates and the Senegal. See UN Water (2010).

energy. The energy crisis will thus go far beyond the predicted explosion of petrol prices. It marks the end of the cycle of cheap fossil fuels (petrol and gas). Without taking sides in debates about the origin of the climate crisis (whether or not it is linked to human activity), it becomes clear that it will be necessary to manage effects which are incontestable and which are directly linked to the simultaneous acceleration of gas emissions and global warming.

If nothing is done in the short term, from 20 to 30 per cent of all living species could disappear within a quarter of a century.[11] The level of the seas and their acidity have increased dangerously and between 150 to 200 million climate refugees may be expected by the middle of the twenty-first century.[12]

Researchers have located five guilty trends which have also recently been the object of a United Nations report:[13] change of habitat caused by deforestation; overexploitation of resources; pollution; invasive exotic species (like algae); and climate changes. If nothing is done by 2050, the devastating effects of deforestation (to take but one example) could result in the 'defragmentation' of the forest ecosystems. Or, in other words, the collapse of their present organization and regulation and the elimination of their animal and plant species. It will cost 6 per cent of the world Gross National Product (GNP).[14]

---

11 According to the International Union for Conservation of Nature (IUCN), the most important organization in the world for animal conservation, 16,000 animal and plant species are threatened with extinction.

12 According to UN forecasts.

13 See UN (2010).

14 See European Communities (2008).

To these grave outcomes needs to be added the explosion in the patenting of the means of life, notably alimentary patenting, another sign of the power of the large multinational groups, to such a point that some ecologists have been able to speak, in relation to these practices, of 'bio-piracy'.[15] Is it not necessary, in the shortest possible time span, to stem these infernal logics?

THE MOST UNACCEPTABLE EFFECT:
THE PULVERIZATION OF POLITICAL ACTION

Confronted with the planetary stakes of the crisis, governments find themselves largely overwhelmed and deprived of the means to provide adaptive solutions. Purely national responses in the face of global challenges appear obviously derisory. Moreover, in the battle waged between financial markets on the one hand and governments on the other, the bank oligopoly seems the most likely to emerge victorious.

One effect of the disequilibrium was exposed, during the crisis, by a remarkable *tour de force* on the part of the bank oligopoly—the private debt of the banks, linked to the subprime crisis, has been transformed into a public debt, eliminating government margins for manoeuvre. The shock wave created by the crisis finds its supplementary continuation here—political action is pulverized, leaving the field free for the bank oligopoly to maintain, indeed reinforce, its position at the heart of a totally globalized finance. But the most disastrous consequence for countries is the considerable amounts needed to

---

15 See, for example, the instructive issue of *Alters Echos* 21 (July–August 2010). Available at: http://sd-1.archive-host.com/membres/up/1564780933753572/journaux/AltersEchos-21.pdf

service the debt, a veritable annual tribute that has to be paid to the financial sphere, to the large banks in particular. This is largely the reason for the severe budgetary plans introduced to some extent everywhere in the world.

A Sudden Acceleration of the World Public Debt

The actual amount of the world public debt and, still more, the exceptional rapidity of its growth, can only arouse anxiety and fear for the future. Admittedly, governments needed to avert the devastating effects of an economic and financial crisis of exceptional seriousness. But the counterpart of this flight of public finances nearly everywhere in the world is now before us—the way out has already proved to be explosive on the social and political levels by reason of the budgetary severity currently imposed on a great number of countries.

Worse, the very process of rehabilitating public finances could lead, as we will see, to a new world crisis.

In December 2009, the world public debt was valued at 3.59 T$ according to the web counter of the *Economist*. The same source forecast, with an accuracy based on currently approved budgets, a debt of 4.1 T$ by the end of 2012. These sums are frightening, but even more so is their extremely rapid evolution. The OECD predicted that the 30 most advanced countries would see their debt increase to 100 per cent of their GDP in 2010, a doubling in 20 years.[16]

Further, Moody's agency, while corroborating this data at the end of November 2009, insists that there will be a rapid acceleration of this evolution because the world public debt rose

---

16 We consider a threshold of indebtedness of 90 per cent of the GDP to be critical for a country. Beyond this threshold it becomes very difficult to master the debt burden.

by 45 per cent between 2007 and 2010—a hike of 1.53 T$ over a very short period indeed! This latter sum represents (when inflation is taken into account) a hundred times the cost of the Marshall Plan raised after the war by the United States to aid the reconstruction of Europe!

The boom in public indebtedness is thus explosive because of the exponentially growing burden it imposes on the public finances of every country. The solutions brought by historical experience to reduce it appear today to be either not up to the task or just so many dead ends.

Could we imagine, for example, a challenge to or a total repudiation of the debt on the part of one or several developed countries?[17] The considerable systemic effects in the financial sphere of such a solution lies beyond the scope of our imaginings—it would be much worse, for example, than the Lehman Brothers effect. A less radical solution could be the reconstruction of certain debts.[18] This path, though widely

---

[17] A country like Argentina, on 23 December 2001, had to repudiate its debt. That day, its parliament voted to default on payment and to suspend reimbursement of all state debts. In February, the country abandoned the fixed parity between the peso and the dollar and converted all of the contracts and borrowings drawn up in dollars into pesos. In 2005, the government decided to restructure the remaining debt—the securities not yet honoured then lost 65 per cent of their value. In 2010, 20 per cent of the debt still remained to be honoured.

[18] Romain Rancière, an associate professor at the École d'économie de Paris, defends the idea that Europe, being a union of sovereign nations, should have 'accepted coping with a risk of default of one of its members'. According to him, it could propose a mechanism of a voluntary restructuring of the sovereign debt as an alternative to a unilateral and messy default: 'In a voluntary restructuring, the creditors choose to exchange their securities against new obligations with

discussed at the time of the crisis of Greek public finances, has also been rejected. Again, as heavily committed creditors of the Greek state, the lobbying of French or German banks may be behind this, their actions relayed by their respective governments to avoid such a scenario.

Can we then conceive of a return of inflation, as some people suggest? We know that inflation is an effective means of lightening the burden of indebted countries. But this path has been closed off since the liberalization of the financial sphere and the independence of the central banks. Has not their mission been fundamentally to preserve the internal value of their currency? In order for this path to be opened, it would be necessary to go back on 40 years of neoliberal thought and practice . . .

There, therefore, remain two traditional solutions: growth; and taxation.

The return of growth does indeed allow a reduction of deficits and a recourse to borrowing. A durable and autonomous economic recovery in the industrialized countries is still not on the agenda. According to IMF forecasts, the growth rates in the developed countries for 2010 were only 1.3 per cent (1.5 per cent in the United States, 0.3 per cent in the Euro-zone, 0.9 per cent in Great Britain and 1.7 per cent in Japan). These perspectives confirm the idea of a very slow growth in these countries, consequently rendering them incapable of even slightly redressing their public finances. This is one of the things that explain the substantial increase of the world public debt in 2010.

---

generally a below par rating and an extension of the maturity of securities' (*Le Monde de l'économie*, 10 May 2010).

The last solution is to increase taxes and to cut down budgetary expenditure. But it would be necessary to do so drastically and over a long period. Here, the risks are clear not only at the political and social level (how could such an implacable severity be justified in the face of a faulty world bank system grown more arrogant through its profits?) but also on the economic level. In vigorously sapping households through taxes, the risk is that growth is once more quashed by consecutive losses of buying power.

This latter path has, nevertheless, been adopted by the governments of the developed countries which pretend to believe that it is practicable. The media hype multiplies in this direction, by promising a return to normality within swift time limits. But the financial markets are not fooled and the spreads[19] on the interest rates of the most exposed countries remain strained.

These solutions, or pseudo-solutions, are not really anything of the sort and will lead countries into a dead end. Admittedly, there still remains recourse to the IMF which, for its part, once again demands (a bad sign!) an increase in its resources. But we can well see that the recourse to this international fund poses enormous problems due to the sums that would have to be allocated when the intervention is for a developed country, one belonging, what is more, as would be the case with Greece, to the Eurozone. The markets then quickly become highly anxious and react very negatively.

---

19 The spread, which generally measures a difference in interest rates, here measures the difference between interest rates obtained by a borrowing country on the financial market and interest rates of borrowing of the country which has obtained the lowest rates (today, Germany).

How then could governments get away from being so dependent on the financial markets and the bank oligopoly? One response, perhaps, consists not in suppressing the financial markets but in eradicating international speculation while smashing the power of the bank oligopoly.

The Keenness of the Confrontation with Political Power

The history of capitalism is dotted with numerous confrontations between political power and financial power, especially in the monetary field. Since the liberalization of the financial sphere happened around 40 years ago, an initial monetary upheaval occurred in September 1992 when speculation had wanted to bring down the project of a single European currency. This attack had, at the time, the result of the departure of British currency from the European Monetary Union (EMU) and the withdrawal of Great Britain from the processes and construction of the euro.

In the wake of its victory, speculation sought on two occasions (in December 1992 and in July 1993) to attack other European currencies, among them *in fine* the franc. But this time unsuccessfully. Franco-German solidarity, at the time, was strong enough to allow the Banque de France to arrange sufficient currency to repel the particularly violent attacks thanks to the amount of resources committed. This stinging failure calmed the bulk of the speculative forces for the next 16 years.

But what was the fundamental reason for these attacks? The speculation was unleashed following the refusal of the Bundesbank to coordinate interest rates across the two shores of the Atlantic, while the United States had entered into recession during the first half of 1992. Faced with the German refusal, the speculators, as well as the American State Department, understood that the single currency then being constructed could act as a weapon against the domination of the dollar. The American authorities then implicitly gave the green light to the unleashing of speculative forces to put a check on the construction of the EMU.

The context at the end of 2009 was very different. The world underwent a major financial crisis and every country was impacted, admittedly to varying degrees. Although the majority of countries in the Eurozone, even before the crisis, had experienced more or less depleted public finances, these countries consented, during 2009, to make important budgetary efforts, both to recapitalize the defaulting banks and to revive their economies, worsening their deficits still further. This was a veritable godsend for the financial actors who had been obliged to record strong falls in their stock exchange capitalizations and/or sometimes very significant financial losses.

Not only have the largest banks returned, from the first half of 2009, to profit from participating in underwriting syndicates of state borrowings whose soaring levels were the result of the crisis but, what is more, their market activities took off better than ever, thanks in the main to the destabilization of the exchange markets and the renewed rising volatility of exchange rates (the source of strong speculative profits). In short, the temptation to attack the weakest links of the Eurozone once more became very strong. All the more so because the means which the speculative forces had at their disposal were without common measure in relation to those at the beginning of the 1990s when financial globalization was only in its infancy. Henceforth, the monetary and financial markets were integrated on a world scale, and the principal bank and finance groups acted over the whole of their divisions. What is more, thanks to the financial crisis, enormous liquidities, as we have seen, have been spread by the central banks that are once more seeking high financial profits. To which it is necessary to add very low interest rates which in turn authorize considerable leveraging.

Should we then be amazed that in December 2009 a monetary offensive of great breadth was launched against the euro, taking as its initial trigger the difficulties of the refinancing of the Greek public debt on the financial markets? Here, too, it is clear that considerable resources were mobilized by speculative forces. Not only had the cost linked to the risk of default by Greece (CDS) strongly crept up but the euro saw its value lowered by around 15 per cent in just a few weeks.

Considering the slowness of the European response and the difficulty of its focusing on the rescue of the Greek public finances, the speculative forces could, it seemed, only be encouraged to pursue their offensive against the European currency at the slightest alarm. They risked taking a malign pleasure in successively bursting the balloons of public debt in the Eurozone. They had the means to do so and spontaneously coordinated them.

Moreover, the intervention of the IMF in Greece in March 2010 confirmed that the credibility of the Eurozone was affected. In spite of the accord reached for a European Monetary Fund (EMF), we knew that Germany would not want to display unfailing solidarity should the situation severely deteriorate. The speculation would therefore have every interest in pursuing its domino game as long as the assertion of an unwavering European political will did not intervene. In other words, the political stake for the Europeans was to take a truly significant step towards an economic government of the Eurozone at the risk of an explosion in a perhaps none-too-distant future.

In short, did this not offer a major occasion in which to shape a counter-offensive and turn round the relation of forces with respect to the financial markets? This stake quite clearly went beyond European frontiers and questioned more broadly the relations between global finance and the unity of nations. From this point of view, the responses brought by the four meetings of the G20 appeared quite insufficient because they left unchanged the logics of coverage formation and therefore of speculative funds.

WALL STREET, THE PROPAGATOR OF THE SHOCK WAVE

Since the middle of the 1990s, the moment when the monetary and financial markets became global, it should be underlined that *financial markets have ceased to be places for the financing of business, even though this is still their main function. The net issuing of shares has become effectively non-existent or negative in the majority of developed countries.* By net issues should be understood in an absolutely classical way the whole of the resources provided at the time of the issues on the primary market (when entering the stock exchange or at the time of capital increases) and not so much the resources withdrawn from it (withdrawal of quotation, payment of dividends, redemption of shares).

This net-sell off varies from country to country, but it is especially negative for the United States. In these conditions, what purpose can the stock exchange still serve? The role of 'stock exchange shares' should here be clearly distinguished from the broader one of 'financial markets', like Wall Street, where 'stock exchange groups' like NYSE Euronext, the most important among them, act. They manage the platforms in which the hyper-power of globalized and liberalized finance is expressed.

Several recent works have clearly shown that the 'stock exchange shares' of the main developed countries, especially of the United States, no longer fulfil their function of financing the real economy (see Graph 1).[20]

The net issues of shares by businesses in the Eurozone have been maintained at a very low level since the end of the first half of 2001. The weak recourse to financing by the issuing of shares is explained by the fact that the cost of other types of financing (credit, bonds) is more favourable. Businesses privilege the policy that aims to satisfy shareholders by limiting the creation of new shares and thus increasing the benefits per share.

This increase in the recourse to bank credit in the United States has been more than compensated by the lowering of the net issuing of shares by businesses. Indeed, the net issues of shares are negative and reached -8.62 T$ in 2004, representing a record level of share buy-back. The policy of buying back shares, associated with recourse to bank debt, is aimed, via the effect of leveraging, at satisfying the shareholders by increasing their benefit per share (see Graph 2).

---

20 Among these works one could call attention to: Patrick Artus, Jean-Paul Betbèze et al. (2008: 23); Elena Stancanelli, Guillaume Chevillon et al. (2005); Jean-Marc Lucas (2007: 7–36); Focus 2 État-Unis: comptes financiers au deuxième trimestre; Frédéric Lordon (2010); and Dominique Plihon (1999).

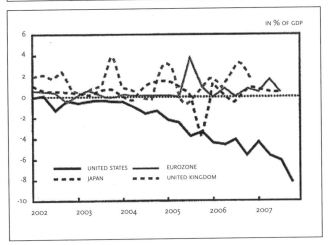

SOURCE: Datastream and Natixis

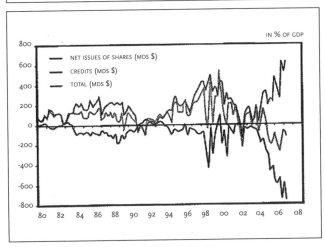

SOURCE: Federal Reserve of the United States

Apart from the role of financing, which they have lost, stock market shares normally fulfil two other functions: the evaluation of companies by a comparison of the supply and demand of shares; and the possibility of bringing together companies by merger or acquisition, notably by the exchange of shares. But is the stock exchange really necessary for this? We doubt it.

Indeed, rates on the stock exchange have been ever more volatile since the middle of the 1990s. This was, first of all, the case with the dot-com bubble; then with the endless crises which have continued since the sub-primes crisis. Finally, these rates have lost any correspondence with the intrinsic value of companies. This means that the more the volatility of a rate is raised the more it feeds speculation, which in turn leads to the rise in what so many observers have called the casino economy. Then the function of the bringing together of companies, by way of the OPE (Offre publique d'echange) or the OPA (Offre publique d'achat), is not the exclusivity of stock exchange mechanisms. The immense majority of mergers, acquisitions or partial business transfers is done outside the stock exchange.

But then, what is the real function of the stock market share today? The most important element is probably *its role as a transmission channel of the financial norm*. The achievement of the financial norm that investors fix on businesses forces the directors to combine in a joint way two types of shares: fast capital gains on speculator rates; and payment of increased dividends. In this way 'stock market shares' no longer fulfil their essential function—to finance business. At the same time, they are the propagators of a norm of unsustainable profitability for the real economy. From that moment, they demonstrate their uselessness and even their harmfulness. But that is not all.

The finance markets are animated by very powerful private actors, the *brokerage firms*, whose role is not only to manage share quotations but also to offer a whole range of products and services. Among the latter should be noted the quotation of derivatives, as well as the services accruing to the markets by mutual agreement with these same products. These products are then, as we saw in the previous chapter, the direct cause of international financial instability and market speculation.

The brokerage firms are therefore at the centre of the functioning of financial markets but also one of their most serious derivatives.

Let's pause for a moment to look at the NYSE Euronext, the most important stock market group in the world. It operates simultaneously on the stock exchanges in New York (Wall Street), Paris, Amsterdam, Lisbon and Brussels. NYSE Euronext brings together several European stock exchange indexes and is a great platform for the exchanges of shares. Two thirds of its turnovers are benefits of negotiation—the execution and management of transactions on derivatives and in cash (shares, bonds, futures contracts, warrants, options, interest rate derivates and so on). In this way the group operates in six share markets (two in the United States and one each in Belgium, France, the Netherlands and Portugal). NYSE Euronext equally manages NYSE Liffe, one of the premier markets in derivatives in Europe and the Second World-derived market in exchange value. The geographical distribution of its sales is as follows: United States 69.6 per cent; Europe 30.4 per cent. The power of this stock market group is thus considerable. It animates Wall Street as well as other financial markets. It is the pivot on which the bank oligopoly is supported to run its operations.

Yet the power of this stock market group is today slightly challenged by the appearance of alternative platforms of financial shares exchanges, notably since 1 November 2007, the date of the application of the European directive concerning markets in financial instruments. The main argument of the new platforms of exchange is their lower tariff compared with traditional markets.[21]

Finally, these platforms, and the main one among them, Euronext, are consequently the essential dealing centres for liberalized and globalized finance. Along with stock market shares (which no longer fulfil their function of financing the economy), they are, in reality, the channel by which shareholder value is propagated, a veritable infectious centre whose disastrous effects (highly organized or negotiated by mutual agreement) on the real economy we have already seen—they are the transmission channel of a speculative bubble managed by the bank oligopoly and whose effect is a destabilization of the world monetary and financial system that has become unacceptable and catastrophic. Then why should one still need to endure a world with Wall Street? Is it not time to revise the financing circuits of the world economy in a fundamental way? We are convinced that it is and that the moment has come to prepare the ground for this construction.

---

21 The three principal competitors of the NYSE Euronext group, namely Bats Europe, Chi-X and Turquoise, or even Tradegate, are beginning to gain not inconsiderable parts of the securities market.

CONCLUSION

There is no denying that a confrontation between two orders of logics, one financial, the other political, has become inevitable. On the one hand, a liberalized finance and its increasingly powerful oligopolistic core, with its own codes and values, encounters virtually no obstacles in its path. Institutional shareholders, with their increasingly excessive demands for financial profitability, disrupt the business world and profoundly change the relations of work by a financial pressure that has become intolerable. Admittedly, booms and scandals have peppered the expansion of this financial sphere, but the adaptation of new prudent rules following the financial crisis, and the reinforcing of the regulating authorities, aim only at palliating the mishaps which are just judged to be regrettable.

On the other hand, democratic societies subject to untenable levels of public debt see a succession of alternating political majorities, often with strong fluctuations, expressing profound dissatisfaction (as is attested moreover by the lasting installation of nationalist extremisms). The political and economic norm, subjected to the ideology of ultra-liberalism, blocks genuinely alternative projects. When one does appear it is limited to 'accompanying' the movement of economic globalization that is considered inevitable. In the end, the only solution would be to 'adapt oneself' to this new deal through 'indispensable reforms'.

How do we set up an effective oppositional force and a credible counter-project? The very concrete stake is to confront the sort of finance whose power is so well symbolized by Wall Street, as well as the excesses and bad habits at the origin of which has unfortunately propagated the dissolution of a whole series of values, notably ethical and moral.

PART 2

OPENING THE BREACH:
A WORLD WITHOUT WALL STREET

What will happen when the next systemic shake up occurs? What consequences of the fragmentation of economic tissues and the loss of ethical, moral or political values can we fear if violent social explosions are unleashed? The worst scenarios are a lot easier to imagine since the inability of political leaders to grasp the current stakes now renders them that likely. A humanity that renounces reason and abandons ethics loses the right to exist.

The current impasse is striking. It is a strong reason to encourage us to open a breach in the wall against which we are being thrown. Seeking alternative paths has become an intellectual and political necessity. A space has to be opened up to reveal routes less dark than those which are foretold. As far as we are concerned, there still exists a different horizon, an alternative route—a world without Wall Street. This idea is defensible.

As has been explained, Wall Street, and especially its principal platform NYSE Euronext, at once condenses, in a formidable way, a space of speculative play and a transmission channel of the financial norm. It is no longer, as one might have expected, a market for financing the real economy. To want a world without Wall Street is not simply to attack a symbol and a platform of exchange. It is, rather, to attack the causes at the source of the current global crisis—the ultra-power of a liberalized finance and the insane demands of shareholder value.

So, another utopia? Yes, if it constitutes the stages of a radical transformation and allows a way out of the crisis other than war. No, if it simply prolongs the destructive logics of the planet and of life.

This utopia assumes, above all, a long-term vision which constitutes a breach with the current intellectual make-up of economists but also, unfortunately, with the majority of political leaders.[1] The dogmas of economic liberalism, if they are

---

1 On this question, a very delicate one for the social-democratic parties, we have been able to note a light inflexion of the French Socialist Party. Although until the present the question of neoliberal financial globalization has always been absorbed in a constrained rather than prioritized way, the text of the National Convention of 27 April 2010 grappled with it right away, forced to do so no doubt by the crisis, by underlining the depth of the crisis as a crisis of civilization. But it should be added that the text is almost silent on the causes of the crisis (liberalization of the financial sphere, the rise in shareholder value). Since then, the responses to the crisis could only be limited, and were not indicated by a rupture of logic in financier practices, even though this was imperative. The notable exception, the Parti de Gauche in France, is the only one to have diagnosed the ultra-power of liberalized finance and put in evidence questions linked to shareholder value. See the party's website for 'Lignes d'horizon pour l'élaboration du programme: repères et ruptures' (1 December 2009. Available at: www.debats-ouverts-a-gauche.org/?p =60).

to be seriously brought into question, remain no less enduring within economic practice. The paths towards a concrete alternative therefore lead through a completely different conception of the regulation of the economy, from the equitable sharing of wealth and the lasting development of the planet.

Concrete measures extended in time, carried along by political and ecological projects that are new and radical by reason of their priorities, are needed next: a renewable and rational use of natural resources along with the recovery by countries of sovereignty over these resources; the halting of monocultures and the reclamation of peasant agriculture; ratification and the deepening of the Kyoto and Bali climate agreements. This has to entail a participative conception of the state as well as a demand for human rights in all their dimensions, whether individual or collective.[2]

At the heart of this new utopia (which must be concrete) is a conception of the economy which must absolutely cease to be under the domination of the financial markets. These, having been allowed far too much elbow room, have demonstrated their incapacity for self-regulation, and are dangerous too. In order to change the deal and be consistent, it will be necessary to act over a very wide palette of political action, going from the planetary global to a territorialized local.

An essential key to this change is the recasting of the system of how the world economy is financed. We now need to assure it of a fresh stability, at once monetary and financial. Monetary, through new international rules on the formation of interest and exchange rates, prefiguring in the long term a currency on an international scale *conceived as a common good of*

---

2 On this fundamental point, see Houtart (2008).

humanity. Financial, *by abolishing the current role of financial markets* which *have completely ceased* to fulfil their role in the financing of business.

Finally, a generalization of democracy will be redeployable in all institutions—and not just in the political sector—in an economic, monetary and financial frame that is stable.[3] It will become possible to conceive of a participatory democracy at the very heart of the economic system, in business, with, in particular, a recasting of property rights in joint stock companies. The abolition of financing sources of a speculative nature will then help open up the path towards a new sharing of wealth and power, and assist in prefiguring a new relation towards money and power for the world's citizens.

---

3 I am here touching on the ideas of Jacques Généreux (2009).

THE BREAK: CHANGE THE INTELLECTUAL MAKE-UP
OF ECONOMISTS

At the end of 2009, in an article published on the front page of *Le Monde*, Jean-Claude Trichet, President, European Central Bank, recognized that the crisis had been intersected by 'the irruption of events whose gravity had not been foreseen'.[1] Trichet hammered home his point by recalling that 'economic reality has from one week to the next confounded the analyses and projections of the most tested models'. He denounced the sort of economic thought that has enjoyed too much confidence in the 'paradigm of equilibrium'. And he cited Hyman Minsky, John Maynard Keynes and Frank Knight as authors to whom we should refer more often in order to understand better situations of financial instability.

What an admission and what an attack upon the whole of neoclassical modelling! One might simply think that he is

---

1 Interview of Jean-Claude Trichet by Pierre-Antoine Delhommais and Arnaud Leparmentier. Available at: http://www.bis.org/review/ r091119b.pdf

not going far enough in his denunciation of standard economic thinking and the still prevailing neoliberalism. He does not, for example, criticize the economy of financial markets at all. Today totally liberalized, they are located where the speculative forces (already very powerful) were strengthened in ever greater proportions precisely when the crisis struck.

Let us, therefore, see what successive explanations 'standard economists'—those whose thought arises doctrinally from neoliberal thought—have been able to give of the crisis. Bringing to light the fundamentalism of this way of thinking will allow us more effectively to make clear its limits and currently devastating effects, not simply in the academic spheres but also in economic practices.

It will then remain for us to show the conditions for a change of intellectual paradigm, the premises of which we perceive among a certain number of economists who, moreover, are trying to organize themselves institutionally.[2] This change of paradigm—which is now beginning—is one of the preliminary and absolutely necessary conditions in imagining a new 'concrete utopia', both for the planet and its citizens.

---

[2] Among foreign examples might be mentioned the British initiative of creating the International Initiative for Promoting Political Economy (IIPPE), whose objective is to promote a new political economy in a critical and constructive relation with the dominant current and alternative heterodox approaches. In France, a new association of economists, the AFEP (Association française d'économie politique), was created in December 2009 with a similar aim, taking up a first-ever attempt at organization initiated by Jacques Généreux's 'Manifeste pour l'économie humaine' (2000), at the time supported by 300 economists from 30 countries.

Those economists obsessed with economic theory, having realized the extent of the current crisis after systematically underestimating it or not having seen it coming at all, are now preoccupied with its treatment by means of precepts that are often delivered in a peremptory way. A more modest and more critical overview on their part of their theoretical presuppositions would be more suited to the actual situation. This would probably allow them to apprehend better the systemic links observed during the financial crisis and in effect even today.

First of all, one can only be struck by the retrospective underestimation of the extent of the crisis. The IMF economists, in February 2008, estimated global losses of assets linked to the crisis of subprimes at $400 billion. A year later, the same estimate had reached 4,000 billion—ten times more and that too only in the case of American assets![3] Should one not then be alarmed about these gigantic errors or even of these hesitations in recognizing the extent of the crisis? To what is this blindness and reluctance due?

After such errors, one might have thought that the amplitude of the crisis would have prohibited recourse to the usual explanations of the so-called standard approach in economy, even if it might here and there be partially correct.

Some observers and economists were content to affirm that the crisis began with the fall of Lehman Brothers until then considered 'too big to fail'. The New York bank collapsed in September 2008, provoking the all-too-familiar panic we

---

3 See the declaration of the director of the IMF in *Les Échos* (28 January 2009).

have all experienced. This explanation which, quite evidently, reflects one part of the truth, leads its authors to a singular proposition—the dismantling of the largest banks to favour a more healthy 'competition' between them. One of the catchwords of standard economic thought was thus put forward and constituted, by its reference alone, 'the' best therapeutic response to the crisis.

Another more subtle and less summary reading essentially interprets the crisis as one of liquidity. This explanation condemns the role of central banks which favoured unrestrained credit. The American Central Bank then stands accused for the fact that, since 2001 and the events of the World Trade Centre, it gave very low interest rates, going down as far as 1 per cent. These terms favoured an expansion of credit that became uncontrollable, and continued for the next few years. By the end of 2006, this excess of liquidity, combined afterwards with a rise in interest rates, was the cause of the crisis of confidence among the banks. In August 2007 the world monetary markets became jammed and provoked a financial and economic crisis. Once again, this explanation provided a partial description of the crisis but was not completely satisfying. 'The excess of liquidity', and therefore of currency, was the shock argument of monetarist thinking grappling to explain the crisis. Then monetarism is nothing other than the monetary assigning of neoliberal thinking.[4]

---

[4] As Gilles Dostaler quite rightly noted: 'If what has been called monetarist inflexion succeeded Keynsian politics, it was in 1968 that the expression of Monetarism was forged. As usual, the current of thought it expresses was born well before then. Monetarism is often considered to be the first vehicle of neoliberalism' (2000: 71–87).

One then arrives at the most widespread standard interpretation, which appears explicitly in the explanations of the
G20 and which is practically central among all of the inter-
pretations of the crisis. The origin of the crisis was to be found
in 'excessive risk taking' on the part of a certain number of
actors. Among them, of course, were the traders, whose activities in the future, we were told, should be supervised. And
then there were the banks which, by reason of the risks they
took with their own funds (invested in structured products
which in the end were found to be toxic), saw their balance
sheets deteriorate, entailing a 'credit crunch' that was fatal to
growth.

The taking of excessive risks is, of course, one element
to be taken into account in the way in which the crisis consol-
idated itself. But, for standard thinking, this element is
absolutely crucial, because it puts in play another key concept—that of 'equilibrium'. With excessive risks caused by the
behaviour of certain actors, the markets could no longer be
in 'equilibrium'. Initially, the price of assets took off in a
movement of euphoria, thereby forming the boom. Thereafter these booms could only shatter and the price of assets
fall, entailing a financial and economic crisis. From that
moment on, standard economic thought recommended a new
regulation which consists of introducing 'stimulations'
(another keyword in this way of thinking) which might modify
the behaviour of the instigators of excessive risks—in this
case, the traders and banks. Henceforth, equilibrium having
returned, the markets will once more become efficient.

As a complement to this central approach, the 'cycle' theory sought to give a historical varnish to the standard explanation. Capitalism, it is said, has throughout its history

experienced cyclical processes of booms followed by busts. What is happening today should therefore not be overestimated. We have certainly experienced a rather more significant boom than the others and, in the end, not surprisingly, it burst. This literature explains to us more precisely that the dot-com boom formed in the United States from 1996 was followed by a real-estate boom which collapsed with the crisis of subprimes. There will be other booms, too, in the future which too will burst in their turn. Therefore we should not be unduly alarmed by this process.

To sum up. Standard economic thinking has today developed round two key concepts: competition and equilibrium. Economists are divided into two groups according to the emphasis they privilege. Thus, economists of equilibrium work more on the theoretical foundations of general equilibrium. For them, the essential point is to demonstrate that a social optimum really corresponds to the equilibrium of the markets.[5] As for economists who privilege the concept of competition, they seek imperfections in the market and then try to reduce them as far as they can. But they all agree about the way to return either to equilibrium or to favour further competitive processes. By supporting their arguments on a theory of information in which informational asymmetries between economic agents would play a great role, it is a matter of

---

[5] Adair Turner, president of the FSA (Financial Service Authority, the regulating body of the British financial market), takes the opposite view to this vision by affirming that it is up to the regulator to fix the limits of the market's social utility in a legitimate way, because it cannot attain 'optimum equilibrium', or demand the reinforcement of the appropriate funds from banks, or again institute taxes on financial flows.

'encouraging' the agents to behave in such a way that either the equilibrium of the market is recovered or that the competition is the purest or most perfect possible.[6] The banks, only those which were liquid, will recover their financial health once their balance sheets are audited; the others, those which were insolvent, will vanish or be nationalized. It is therefore not necessary to be overly worried.[7] Finance has not gone mad.

To this vision—which takes micro-economic behaviour effectively into account—we need to add a macro-economic point about the role of the central banks, which did not know how to prevent the formation of booms in the price of assets (on stock exchange quotations or American real estate). At no moment is this way of thinking capable of prioritizing either the systemic character of the crisis or the effects of the contagion linked to derivatives issued by the financial industry.

What is the origin of this neoliberalism which adorns itself in the virtues of competition and equilibrium, and which promotes solutions in terms of regulation? One can go back to 1947, to when the Mont-Pèlerin Society was founded in Lausanne by economists like Friedrich Hayek and Milton Friedman but also by journalists, jurists and other intellectuals. Their idea? To think the future of the world for the next 30–40 years in terms of the 'liberalization' of the economy. These economists projected onto the future a vision in which the state would, in some way, disappear, because its interventions were ineffective in treating economic questions seriously. It

---

6 For a good synthesis of standard thinking about the financial crisis, see Tirole (2008).

7 Martin Wolf (2009).

was also a matter of struggling against the threats posed by 'state control' of all sorts, Keynsian and socialist as much as communist.

In short, the economy, especially the financial sphere, had to be liberalized. This sphere was indeed, in their eyes, the key device. Then, according to the same logic, it would be necessary to liberalize the other sectors, notably those of public services and general interest. The years from 1950 to 1960 would thus be the years in which this fundamental idea was intellectually fermented. It was during this period that the doctrine of neoliberalism was forged. It so happened that this doctrine encountered opportunities in the unfolding of events which allowed it to lend reality to its ideas.

As was discussed in the first chapter, the practical setting up of this economic conception took place in August 1971, with the break with the Bretton Woods accords and the creation, some time afterwards, of floating exchange rates between the major currencies. Following the precepts of this neoliberalism, exchange rates were henceforth determined by the laws of supply and demand. But, as a result, *it was necessary as soon as possible to protect businesses from exchange risks. This led to the creation of futures markets to immunize export or import businesses.* These futures contracts represented the first blooming of the market in derivatives which would become the centre of the current crisis.

The other stage, equally absolutely essential for neoliberalism as it increasingly became anchored in economic life, would occur at the beginning of the 1980s with the liberalization of interest rates through the creation of vast financial markets. Countries were no longer required to finance their budgetary deficits by printing money, or, in other words, through the monetary financing of public deficits but, on the contrary, through financing on the bond markets. With this new liberalization, a second shock for the real economy followed that of exchange rates. As before, it would be necessary to create coverage products which would allow, it was thought, the system to be restabilized.

It is from that point on that the promotion of 'financial innovation' by neoliberal thought can be understood. In reality, behind this apparently attractive formula was hidden the unbridled development—over the next two decades—of an industry in derivatives. This particular innovation was thus an integral part of the process of liberalization. No liberalized finance without a market in derivatives!—such is the conception of contemporary neoliberalism. This is why among the reforms proposed by the G20, whose inspiration remains fundamentally marked by this re-branded liberalism, it is not at all a matter of suppressing derivatives but only of 'organizing their markets better', as they are judged not to be very transparent, and to favour excessive risk taking.

One can hardly ask theorists who have made the concepts of equilibrium and the market the cornerstones of their intellectual construction to think otherwise. They have founded their beliefs on the absolute efficiency of market mechanisms to resolve all economic problems.[8]

---

8 As Alain Supiot said just as well about economists, 'Scientistic dogmatisms do not recognize themselves as such and are completely impermeable to any sort of external criticism. This is their strength, but also their weakness, when they find themselves, as the neoliberal doctrine does today, caught by the reality principle. The political and economic elites which incarnate it are then incapable of understanding why the world slips away from under their feet' (2010: 93).

Other less standard explanations appear a little more convincing. They take us back to the beginning of the 1980s and propose, as the cause of the crisis, insufficient demand, the origin of which in turn was a new distribution of revenues. According to this explanation, with the diminishing role of wages in added value, we enter an era of under-consumption by wage earners and simultaneously an over-accumulation of capital by reason of an increase in dividends. By placing the emphasis on inequality of income, one is here very close to the theses of Marxism.

A whole range of explanations for the financial crisis thus mobilizes arguments of over-accumulation on the one hand and a crisis of demand on the other to insist on the 'real' factors for the financial crisis. Why have these latter approaches not had the force of conviction which could have reversed (at least intellectually) the standard explanations? Two reasons can undoubtedly be seen in this, one of which is material, the other intellectual.

In the balance of powers that oppose it to heterodox thought, 'standard' thought often benefits from considerable financial support. Especially from the largest banks. For not only do the banks profit from the advice given by a good proportion of the university economists but they also contribute generously to the financing of research projects, or, better still, provide the initial capital for the creation of research foundations. Thus in 2007, the principal European centre in standard economy, the Toulouse School of Economics (TSE), raised €60 million to create a foundation, half of which was provided by the banks and the other half by the French state.

But the other reason for the weakness of heterodox approaches is probably down to their own insufficiency. By insisting too much, for example, on the 'real' factors of the financial crisis (under-consumption, over-accumulation), these approaches hide the intrinsically 'financial' aspects of the current crisis. Instead of seeing in the deformation of how added value is divided a direct effect of the rise of shareholder value (spread by new financial investors), they were too soon content with the good old Marxist explanations relating to inequalities necessarily engendered by the relation between capital and labour. The radically new character of the current financial crisis was then lost from view with, on the one hand, the creation of derivatives whose outstanding debts and volumes of transaction are literally breathtaking and, on the other, the emergence of worldwide financial groups, highly speculative in their market activities and whose demands with regard to yield are, quite literally, insane.

All things taken into consideration, it is necessary to break not only with the intellectual make-up of standard economists but also to take the critique made by heterodox economic thinking one notch further.

THE CHANGE OF INTELLECTUAL PARADIGM

The profession of the economist (largely dominated by standard economic thought) is obviously under scrutiny as to the pertinence and social utility of its scientific production when confronted with a world financial, economic, ecological and social crisis. Not to have anticipated the crisis—on behalf of this way of thinking—and not having anything much to say about it strongly contributes towards discrediting the discipline.

Economists are above all reproached for their incapacity to make reality such as it is intelligible and, in a crisis situation, with their inability to diagnose it without complacency. This step would obviously be the only one that could allow the construction, in a credible way, of the elements of a scenario offering a way out of the crisis.[9]

The major crisis we are currently experiencing offers, as everyone can see, the most exemplary illustration of the blindness of economists.

Confronted with this negligence, should the profession as a whole be accused or only a part of it? In fact, economists are divided into several analytical streams. Should we for all that put them in the same boat? Or rather, is it not necessary to highlight the limits of a particular type of approach, one which however has assumed prominence at the heart of economic analysis?

Admittedly, we have already anticipated the response to this question by demonstrating the essential role of neoliberal thought. But what should now be unveiled is the truly hegemonic hold this thought plays in the intellectual and institutional field of the profession. It is in this that this way of thinking manifests an extreme danger not only for the discipline as such but also *in fine* for the whole of society.

An Unacceptable and Dangerous Hegemony

The hegemony today acquired by neoliberal thought has diffused widely through research institutions and higher education. On the theoretical level, it has been consecrated by the neoclassical paradigm (the academic version of neoliberalism)

---

9 Several of the ideas in this chapter were inspired by the intellectual approach of the AFEP, an association currently seeking to more effectively organize the critical approaches to standard economic so as to make them more hard-hitting.

which has, over time, become an obstacle to collective reflection and critical research. This paradigm is the prime obstacle that, as a matter of priority, needs to be attacked.

In real terms, this hegemony is expressed through an eminently unacceptable practice—the presently programmed aim of pluralism at the heart of economic thought and, through it, the disappearance of any real economic debate. The consequence of this ideological domination is expressed by numerous inadmissible professional and institutional practices.

One of the most pernicious of them, and the least known by the greater public, is the promotion of publications in peer-reviewed journals to the detriment of publication in books. The control of the diffusion of learning among economists is thus done so much more easily when a researcher is required to pass under the caudine fork of a peer review. His recruitment, the progression of his career are, in this way, determined only by the articles published in supposedly high-level journals with peer reviewers.[10] It is then enough to establish the list of journals which are open to receive research work and so to control the way their advisory boards are composed.

By then rating these journals, each researcher can easily be evaluated and judged according to his or her intellectual profile. The effectiveness this professional control has had over recent years should be recognized. Neoclassical theory has effectively been diffused at the same rate as the processes of the liberalization and financialization of the economy. Its

---

10 It is very striking to note that, in this discipline, responsibilities in teaching or in administration are never taken into account in career development.

hegemony was definitively affirmed in the 1980s and its so-called scientific representations, for example that of the efficiency of financial markets, reigned practically unchallenged at the time the financial crisis erupted.[11]

At the university level, the increasing power of standard thought has been rendered possible over 30 years only because a very structured fraction of the disciplinary field has confronted a heterogeneous and not-very-well organized multitude which has mostly submitted to this situation, only resisting where it could, sometimes by leaving the discipline and its official networks.

In a theoretical framework which has progressively ossified round concepts of market equilibrium, competition and stimulation, authorized empirical confrontations are limited only to econometric tests—to what can simply be measured and made to fit the equation. The result of these practices is not surprising, and it means the abandonment of all theoretical or methodological debate over the fundamentals of the discipline. The reduction of research to a sample group of techniques, to the detriment of any critical reflection, is what constitutes 'economic science' as a whole, at least at the time of the financial crisis. The current state of dilapidation is therefore hardly surprising.

---

11 The concept of efficiency has been at the centre of asset- and risk-evaluation models: for example, the Capital Asset Pricing Model (CAPM), the Intertemporal Capital Asset Pricing Model (ICAPM) and the Arbitrage Pricing Theory (APT). This concept was proposed by Maurice Kendall in 1953 and then modified by Eugene Fama in 1965. For Kendall, stock market circulation instantaneously integrates available information and equally reflects the fundamental value of the issuing business.

Let us examine the state of the intellectual sites of the discipline. Reduced, as we have just seen, to a set of 'tested' techniques (essentially game theory and econometrics), economic science very quickly tried to enlarge its hegemony by seeking to annex other social sciences. How? By imposing its own evaluation criteria and quantitative tools on them as rigorous signals of scientificity. Instead of seeking a genuine dialogue between disciplines, it has, on the contrary, shown itself to be entirely domineering.

At the time of the financial crisis there was obviously a shock. The crisis very quickly became a crisis of economic thought. 'Economic science' was revealed in the eyes of all to be pitifully incapable of offering a reading of the contemporary world in a way that would illuminate the real causes of the catastrophe. How can one believe then that this 'science' might still nourish, for example, a democratic debate about the scenarios offering a way out of the crisis?

The truth may then appear completely basic. 'Economic science', because it accompanied, first of all, the processes of liberalization of the financial sphere, then the process of financialization of the world economy, finds itself constantly in closest proximity to those political or economic interests that are linked to globalized finance. Consequently, it has been subject to strong pressure from these particular interests.[12]

---

12 In an interview given to *Libération* (2 July 2010), ecologist MP Pascal Cardin denounced the over-representation of financial circles in the EU's institutions. But 'the problem is that the majority of economists who understand financial questions well are either bank economists or academics whose research is partly financed by them. This, in effect, limits the independent character of their analysis. A counter-power able to contest the banks does not exist.'

An Indispensable Change of Paradigm

What can be done so that societies are able to equip them-selves with tools and institutions of knowledge, illumination and ideas which will be useful in public debates about the organization and functioning of the economy? What can be done to escape the growing hold of financial markets and con-sequently the domination of the neoliberal thought that is intrinsically attached to them?

According to Gilles Dostaler:

> Neoliberalism is not an inevitability. The current mutations might not lead to the catastrophe that the neoliberal utopia bears within it. But nothing is cer-tain. There are no laws of history. Its unfolding is the fruit of the balance of powers, between social groups and countries. It is relatively easy to bring to light the weaknesses of neoliberal theses. Several currents of thought, inspired by Marx, institutionalism or Keynes, are successfully employed within it. But it is so much more difficult to turn aside from the path on which almost every country in the world has today embarked . . . It remains to be seen if a new catastrophe, like that of the 1930s, will be needed for history to deliver a positive solution, in conform-ity with the interests of the majority of populations in the world, rather than to those of minorities which ceaselessly enrich themselves. There is no good rea-son to be exaggeratedly optimistic (2000).

The catastrophe Dostaler anticipated and feared has now unfortunately happened and, what is more, the countries of the world have not yet turned away from the path on which they were committed before its occurrence. Therefore, no positive solution is yet in sight.

It is clear today that the financial crisis has not fundamentally changed the economic and financial practices of neoliberal inspiration, even if, paradoxically, neoliberal thought as such has been dealt a considerable body blow. We are therefore in a situation of flux, with a disoriented and discredited economic thought but with economic practices which remain anchored in the old world. One could thus use the image of a lame duck with its head cut off but which continues to run. But for how long?

The moment is therefore favourable to advance along the path of a new intellectual paradigm that must, above all, concern economists. This is a matter of one of those forced transitions that will cause the concrete utopia of a new world to emerge. Indeed, in adhering to neoliberalism, the standard economists have known for 40-odd years how to encourage the idea that society, and consequently the state, should submit to the economy and its natural laws, those of the market and competition, notably in the financial realm. The intellectual failure is now evident and the rules of the game which prevailed during the Trente Glorieuses,[13] the period of prosperity when the nation-states played a great role, must be set as a contrast.

To commit oneself to the path of a new paradigm, it is necessary to redefine, on the one hand, what the status of the new 'economic science' should be in the intellectual field, and,

---

13 The period in France from 1946 to 1975, the 30 glorious years of post-war reconstruction, rapid growth and increasing prosperity, which then to an extent stalled due to the effects of the 1970s' oil crisis (Trans).

on the other, what the new relations between the economy and society should be in the field of practice.

The Status of the New 'Economic Science'

If it is necessary to insist on the core of a new paradigm, it is equally necessary for there to be a place in it, as an absolute priority, for the concept of 'pluralism', for two fundamental reasons.

One, it is a matter of assuring a clear rupture with a hegemonic practice, one that has now become insupportable and unacceptable, that of the growing and unmitigated professional and institutional hold of standard economic thought. Nor is this a question of totally eradicating it so as to replace one hegemonic practice with another. The fundamental idea is to develop a new spirit of tolerance that should never have left the university campuses.

But here it is a matter of going beyond the idea of tolerance proper to all intellectual activities, whether of the natural sciences, the social sciences or others. Pluralism has to be an essential way for the community of economists to think about their social role. It is a necessary practice to expose the interests that seek to instrumentalize it.

It is a secondary matter to favour debates on critical ideas and approaches that alone can advance research on the economic questions and realities faced by our societies, but pluralism must equally be applied to its methods. Purely normative models need to be confronted with other approaches that take into account the fact that the inherent characteristic of the future is the irreducibility of its uncertainty. What is more, one should abandon the idea that economic tools alone are effective in measuring economic facts.

The expression of these conditions must as quickly as possible establish themselves in the economist community. They must be able to be deployed according to three major directions proposed here.

One, the pluralism must be that of theoretical problems and references. The debate about the basic concepts of the economy is indeed far from being closed. Alongside neoclassical thought there exist other fertile and legitimate traditions, the most well known being institutionalism and Keynesianism, Marxism and evolutionism. But others, more recent ones, have an equal claim to being part of this list: the economy of conventions; the social and interdependent economy; the theory of regulation. This diversity must be considered a wealth and not a factor of disciplinary dispersion or impoverishment. Why should it be forbidden to combine different conceptual approaches that are contingent with the studied objects?

It is then necessary to promote the pluralism of methods and points of view. To the extent that the economy no longer comes down to 'economic theory' in the narrow sense of this term (in other words, the standard theory in reality, with the micro and macro economies),[14] there are many other ways and means of advancing economic knowledge. Among them, let us mention the history of economic thought, the history of economic facts, ideas about methodology, economic philosophy and sociology. These approaches need to be considered as totally legitimate and important points of view. It is time to realize that conceptual and theoretical reflection can

---

14 This is the new 'classic' macro-economy which, as a theoretical current, corresponds most narrowly with neoliberalism, with its guru, Robert Lucas.

only be favoured by the precise interaction of questioning that these fields organize.[15]

Finally, pluralism must be inscribed in the opening onto the other disciplines of the social sciences, together with the abandonment of all hegemony on the part of economic thought in relation to other social sciences. In fact, the majority of social sciences have completely lost interest in the economy, which they regard as a discourse apart and about which they have nothing to say. If the paradigm changes, interdisciplinary openings and collaboration with other human and social sciences will once again become possible. Who wants to deny that the economy belongs with the social sciences? Do not the social sciences form a structured and complex field that needs to be enlarged in a balanced way across its various components?

New Relations between the Economy and Society

The intellectual values of what pluralism in economy would signify for both the discipline and the other social sciences have just been set out. But how are these values important for life in society? The response should nevertheless be obvious—by contributing to the political debate at the heart of the city.

This is why, in a time when neoclassical thought is crumbling, some people seek to re-connect with the spirit of the project formerly carried by 'political economy'. From the work of Antoine de Montchrestien up to the end of the nineteenth century,[16] 'political economy' was indeed the term by

---

15 Here I adhere to the general anthropology developed by Jacques Généreux in *La Dissocieté* (2006) and *L'Autre société* (2011).

16 Jean-Baptiste Say was perhaps the first person to introduce a clear separation between the two realms.

which was designated the discipline followed by economists. But, when they wanted to turn it into a scientific work at the beginning of the twentieth century, in the manner of the hard sciences, political economy was transformed into the 'economic sciences'. This change of identity was destined to make one believe that this discipline had become an exact science and that it consequently had nothing in common with politics or with the political sciences. The latter were considered to be so much less rigorous than the economic discipline, as well as being especially burdened with values which could hinder research into economic efficiency.

This dichotomic vision was clearly a snare. There was obviously no unbreachable frontier between the two worlds and there never has been. Economists are very often experts in the service of public powers; politicians, too, often come from the economic world or else are subject to the lobbying of the largest companies.

To look more closely, neoliberal thought, that of Hayek or Friedman, even the critical discourse of Keynes, did not advocate non-intervention or a non-separation between the economy and politics. It is clear—each in his way saw the finalities, the modalities of the state's intervention and the groups one had to privilege. But there was no watertight barrier between politics and economy.

Whatever the expression used to signify the change of paradigm, what then is the theoretical and practical stake in relation to the period which has just passed? In the light of the crisis and its effects, but also of its deep causes, *it is the capacity to increase mastery over the economy through political power*. It is no longer an effort to submit society and the state to private economic interests, especially those of the financial sphere.

Globalization must no longer, in any case, be an argument about still submitting society to the economy. Not only is it necessary to turn round the mechanism at the national level but also, henceforth, we will only be able to advance a new paradigm, and the new practices associated with it, if the mastery of the economic by the political is exercised at all levels of life in society, from the local to the international.

TO ACT: A DIFFERENT CONCEPT OF THE COHERENCE OF POLITICAL ACTION

To conceive of a credible alternative political response in the face of a crisis so global is a challenge. It is necessary to unite in a coherent way both the intellectual pluralism needed for a democratic debate and the organization of plural levels of action which should, normally, follow from it.

The crisis is so profound that it has been possible to refer to a crisis of civilization in its wake. It is not only economic, financial or social but also global and, in the end, political, but this time on a planetary scale. It would therefore be illusory to enclose oneself in fragmentary responses at whatever level, whether national or local, continental or even international. In order for the action taken to be comprehensible to all, a frame and coherence perceptible on every scale of political action is needed.

What is now necessary is therefore an alternative global response, and a definition of the conditions by which it may be set to work. The preceding chapter furnished an initial response—the intellectual make up of economists has to be radically changed. But it proposed a supplementary idea which, as far as we are concerned, is essential. We must recast economic science on a political economy that has recourse to a conceptual and methodological plurality.

This idea should now be expanded across the social and political sciences. It is a matter of making way for an intellectual pluralism which can renew the whole of the field covered by the sciences of society. It is, in fact, this pluralism which can fundamentally nourish a genuinely democratic debate about an alternative project. The encounter between researchers, robust in their expertise, and citizens, robust in their rights, should be an essential democratic moment.

After having made clear the principles upon which this type of encounter can flourish, I will try to indicate the broad themes which can help nourish the democratic debate. I will do so from an essentially economic perspective. Indeed, the project I defend here, at the level of symbol and practice, is above all to build a world without Wall Street.

THE PRINCIPLES OF ACTION

I will now try to outline the conditions required in order to formulate an alternative and credible project. I will set down four principles for discussion which constitute so many prerequisites for a more precise formulation of the themes to be debated in order to advance alternative routes.

First Principle: an Intellectual Posture which Integrates Three 'Neithers' (or What the Alternative Project Should Not Be)

Let us set aside the series of alternative approaches which privilege in a predominant, even exclusive, way one of the only possible paths of political action. It is necessary to fall, in our sense, into neither *globalism* nor *localism* nor, finally, into *nationalism*.

The refusal of globalism[1] should be understood as that of all political propositions which consider reforming the current course of the planet only by action initiated 'from on high'. These approaches regard effective political action as necessarily coming from political summits which are then to be disseminated towards the base. According to this type of approach, a reform of the international institutions of Bretton Woods with a change of world governance, could in itself initiate the greatest changes for every citizen on the planet.

Inversely, localism has no confidence, or rather can no longer have confidence, in actions that come from on high. It can, most particularly, no longer have belief in initiatives from the 'political' sphere, because this sphere lost its credibility long ago as far as the partisans of localism are concerned. This distrust is reinforced by the idea that only action at the base could bring about a change in the mentality of politicians and make them aware of the stakes today. It is therefore necessary to militate for a short-circuiting of distribution and production with the firm conviction that, through this process, which is admittedly indirect but within everyone's grasp, the whole of the economic and political sphere must fundamentally change its logic.

But, the greatest danger, as in the past, is nationalism. To believe that the nation will tomorrow be the essential, even unique, lever of promises of change is once more to prepare

---

1 See Aurélien Bernier (2010).

oneself for a dramatic future. The nationalist scenario appears credible in the current political situation. If violent social explosions should arise in several countries following the lowering of the purchasing power and the development of mass unemployment, contagious effects on a wider scale cannot be excluded. There would then inevitably be a confrontation between financial and economic powers, especially between the world-wide bank oligarchy and white-hot nationalism. This could lead it towards totalitarianism or to the isolationism of identity and security typical of fascism, possibly with armed confrontations between countries. It is consequently indispensable to break with those purely nationalistic visions and consider the nation-state more as a resource for political action than as a finality.

This vision of three 'neithers' encourages us to militate in favour of a pluralism of the fields of political intervention, going from the most territorialized local to the broadest global one, while not, of course, forgetting national and continental levels. Finally, it is a question of composing rather than opposing the pluralism of objects and methods of studies before furnishing each time the substance of democratic debates.[2] A vision of this nature is the opposite of standard economic approaches in which disciplines like those of micro-economy or even the macro-economy remain profoundly marked, sometimes implicitly, by national parameters.[3]

---

[2] As in the physical sciences, although hard science still claims to be exact: 'Our knowledge of the universe . . . is found to be cut out into a series of theories which describe phenomena perfectly in their own terms, but not as linked together' (Fenoglio 2010).

[3] In micro-economy the concept of the 'social optimum' is thus a notion which refers to a national space; in macro-economy the

*Second Principle: the Common Good of Humanity
as a Point of Departure of the Democratic Debate*
The common good[4] of humanity expresses the choice of a
new vision of the world, founded on the system of universal
human and ecological rights. In short, a new world order supported, reinvented and controlled by citizens' movements.

A first step in this direction was taken when the notion of
a 'common patrimony of humanity' was decided for the management of the seas and oceans, the planets and the heavenly
bodies. It comprises four elements: their non-appropriation by
anyone; international management by the United Nations;
the sharing of benefits among all nations; and the exclusively
peaceful use of natural resources.

Another, broader, stage should now be embarked upon to
approach questions as vital as the maintenance of peace and
security in the world, the struggle against hunger, the preservation of the diversity of species, the future of the climate, the

---

notion of a 'world economy' does not exist—the whole theoretical
field is oriented so as to result in recommendations of 'economic
policies' of a national character.

4 There exists an 'official' definition of 'global public goods'—that of
the international financial institutions of Bretton Woods. It was
inspired mostly by the reductionist and ambiguous definition by the
economist Paul Anthony Samuelson—a public good is something
(such as the air, the soil or the water) which economic actors of the
market need to function, without any of these actors knowing how
to produce or to monopolize it. It was then acknowledged that its
regulation (but not inevitably its property or management) should
be entrusted to public power. This definition is negative and does
not prevent excessive commercialization, squandering or pollution
(of the water, of nature, of the earth, etc.).

113

management of natural resources[5] and energy and, as will be revealed in a moment, the consideration of currency as a common good.

The definition of the perimeter of these common goods questions the unlimited exercise of property rights on the one hand, and has to lead us to a supranational juridical representation of the common interests of humanity on the other. International organizations therefore need to play a decisive role in the recognition of these goods.

But the definition of these goods also has the advantage of offering a freedom other than that of the market. In this realm, apprenticeship in cooperation is prioritized over competition.[6] In this sense, common goods favour open technologies, developed and controlled in common rather than proprietary technologies that tend to concentrate powers.

Numerous realizations are already going in this direction and have prompted the formation of transnational alliances: Creative Commons licences; Wikipedia; the free software and free culture movements; shared platforms; bodies of struggle against open-cast mine exploitation; alliances promoting Bem-Viver 'good life' approach; the worldwide movement for sustainable agriculture; the Water Commons; shared gardens; the citizens communication and news projects; and many others.[7]

---

5 See Solange Koné et al. (2008).

6 According to Nobel Laureate Elinor Ostrom : 'Better to encourage cooperation through institutional arrangements that are tailored to local ecosystems than to try to manage everything from a distance'. Thanks to her work, many universities have re-discovered the academic interest in common goods.

7 These alliances could be the basis of a new economy: 'Free and cooperative activity, in networks, founded on gratuity and the

Yet, the question of freedom of access to common goods is still posed in relation to the cost of their preservation, management and development. This means that this freedom of access and use does not necessarily induce gratuity. The municipalization of water management induces financing through taxes of the new skills of collectives; the open and free encyclopaedia Wikipedia functions on the economic model of the gift; the free software movement rests on the idea that the putting in common of some (and only some) source codes benefits the actors of the community, on condition that each of them commits themselves to put their work back into the community.

Finally, on the matter of common resources, it is necessary to attend to the equitable sharing and participation in all the decisions taken on the issue of their access, usage and control. This implies a profoundly democratic approach, as much politically (principles of decentralization, subsidiarity and sovereignty) as economically (the mode of production of common goods reduces dependency on money and the market).

Third Principle: a Plural and Multicultural Actor

Common goods thereby offer a fresh perspective and conceptual approach with already perceptible realizations. But can they be the bearers of an alternative broader project in the future? To pose this question is to envisage the construction of a vast diversified movement, credible and sufficiently long-lasting to change the logic of the system into which the world has at this moment been plunged.

---

pleasure of creating, is more efficient than the old exploitation of minds' (Dostaler and Maris 2009: 136).

As Houtart has observed, the genius of capitalism has often been to transform its contradictions into opportunities; to quote as an example this headline from *USA Today* in 2007: 'How Can Global Warming Make Us Richer?' Will capitalism be able to go as far as to renounce its own principles? Obviously not, and in any hypothesis it would be very naive to believe that it would. Only a new relation of power will succeed in doing so, which does not exclude the possibility of a rallying of certain contemporary economic actors.

What can therefore be the new historical actor, bringing alternative plans? It is obviously plural. It must gather the workers, and more widely the wage earners subject to the stress of shareholder value, landless peasants, indigenous people, the poor of the cities, militant ecologists, migrants, intellectuals linked to social movements and some of the elites increasingly aware of the dangers threatening our planet. The consciousness of belonging to a collective actor is beginning to emerge. Social networks make a great contribution. The convergence of organizations which believe in alternative projects is only in its initial phase and often lacks political relays. Some governments, especially in Latin America, have already created the conditions for alternatives to emerge.[8] The duration and intensity of the struggles of the political and

---

8 At the end of 2003, Latin America entered a period of political mutation crowned with thirteen presidential elections. Since then the majority of governments of the region have placed a priority on projects of regional integration: Mercosur, ALBA, Banque du Sud, Gazodue continental, 'sugar' (as regional currency) and so on. The struggle for another possible world, for another political practice, assumes a concrete and sometimes extreme shape in countries like Venezuela, Brazil and Ecuador.

social actors will depend on the rigidity of the system in place and the intransigence of its protagonists.

To reverse the course of history, these actors would need to be able to meet more, to compare their ideas peacefully and share their cultures—in short, to find collective spaces of expression, as for example in various world forums where a multicultural sensibility should be constituted into a force of proposition for the abolition of patents on knowledge, for the liberation of science from the stranglehold of economic and financial powers and for the suppression of news monopolies.

Fourth Principle: to Break in a Radical Way
with the Current Management of Risk

Risk is a prominent feature of modern societies. The difficulty of managing it leads to problems of increasing complexity which governments will have to deal with, notably in matters of evaluations. In fact, the problem is not only the extent of risk and its probability of occurrence but also the power to evaluate the extent of the damage which would be occasioned if it was to occur.[9]

Many technologies carry such risks—the nuclear indus-try, for example, the GMO or even the nanotechnologies. One could think also of an old example like mad cow disease, or, more recently, the H1N1 (swine flu) virus. The financial crisis has equally brought into the open the risks of a systemic nature which might gravely affect the economic planet.

When such risks materialize or remain only potential, confidence in the public powers is weakened or even shattered.

---

9 On this difficult question of the management of risk one could usefully refer to the special issue of *La Recherche*—'Inventons le futur' (July–August 2010).

Suspicion is then formed among citizens about a connivance between public powers and private interests[10] which then goes on to undermine expertise and its independence. Generally speaking, this loss of confidence is a recent phenomenon. It reflects doubts born from the way in which the crises of the past 20 years, economic or scientific, have been managed.

If the economic and financial spheres should now be the object of regulation, science must without any doubt, in conditions to be determined, equally be the object of social control. We fear far more a risk that is imposed on us without any warning, while we accommodate ourselves more easily to those we have chosen. The recovery of confidence in public powers is vital for democratic debate. It alone can favour a profound dialogue, without ulterior motives, and allow, in an efficient way, the complexity of the problems that are posed to our societies to be approached.

But the situation has grown far more serious, because the way to manage a certain type of risk—financial risk—increasingly eludes governments. With financial liberalization, it has been the markets that intend to mutualize the risk and manage it completely. Mutualization thereby passes through insurance products—the infamous derivatives, whose speculative potential was evident during the financial crisis. Worse, governments fall prey to speculation when they seek to finance themselves

---

10 The lobbying of banks is currently effective because they have a better sight of the markets than do the regulators and a fortiori the politicians. The bankers find themselves in the majority in groups of experts who work, for example, for the European Commission or the Council for Financial Stability. Thus, in Europe, the group on derivatives consists of 34 experts representing the banks and only 10 from the public powers (see the article in *Libération*, 2 July 2010).

through the bondholder markets. In fact, the debt that a state issues becomes the object of insurance contracts, to the benefit of investors who buy public securities. The investors are thus protected against the risk of default by this state.

But it should not be forgotten that these contracts (the CDS) are sold and then bought on the financial market, and that the insurance premiums of these contracts then vary depending on the risk of default represented by a particular state. The insurance premium, still called a risk premium, then serves as a referential to fix the interest rates of future public borrowings. And so, like any financial product, the CDS can be the object of powerful speculative movements. This is the reason for which, in submitting the cost of their public borrowings to the arbitration of the financial markets, countries are more and more enslaved by the yoke of these markets and their speculative movements.

Now the machinery of risk coverage by the financial markets has itself derailed with the financial crisis and countries have not dared, during G20 meetings, to banish it completely. Finally, no individual or institution has any real capacity to manage the risks of our economic system. It is therefore really this infernal machine that must be smashed. A world without Wall Street would be one that must fall back on its feet by eliminating the devastating madness of the liberalized financial markets.

COHERENCE: FROM THE PLANETARY GLOBAL
TO THE TERRITORIALIZED LOCAL

A non-exclusive intellectual posture, the common good of humanity as departure point of the democratic debate, a plural and multicultural actor, a new management of risk—the setting up of these four great principles are thus articulated to prepare the ground, allowing a break with the current system.

It is, first of all, necessary to defend the idea of a world government, something that is needed as soon as possible, round the fundamental stakes of the currency but also, by extension, round the fiscal and environmental stakes. The idea of an economic integration of the large regions of the world comes next, accompanied by a decentralization of international institutions. An in-depth rehabilitation of public services in parallel, especially along with the creation of public financial poles. Finally, it is also necessary to render the circuits of production and distribution a lot shorter.

The world that will emerge at the outcome of this journey will be such that Wall Street will lose its *raison d'être*.

A World Government as Soon as Possible:
Currency, Fiscal Policy, Environment

Confronted with an emergency, this is what we need to think about right at the very beginning of political and citizen intervention on the world scale.

The first point to note is that urgent questions like those of the excess of liquidity, the rising price of raw materials, emissions of CO_2, or even of outsourcing, cannot be controlled at the level of nations or even of a group of nations like the European Union.

This need for extra-national regulation will become even more important if one enlarges the temporal horizon of problems to be resolved through the management of the 'common good of humanity'. The treatment of all these questions on a world scale has now become inevitable.

What should be done? One solution consists in replacing the international institutions, which date from the end of the Second World War (the IMF, WTO, ILO and so on) and which bring together only the developed countries, with genuinely world organizations.[11] These would be open to all countries and would have as their task not only the preservation of the common patrimony of humanity but also the management of its common goods according to democratic principles.

From this perspective, a world government could be formed, to encourage and coordinate the action of these new organizations. It could truly establish its authority only on an indisputable democratic legitimacy resting, for example, on parliamentary representation that would inevitably need to be established on an international scale.

The action of this government could be strongly inspired by a principle set out by Juan Somavia, director general of the ILO. It is a question of the principle of equivalent norms, and he recently set out the possible content:

> The problem is the very strong segmentation of the world normative system. It does not allow for coherence between the various policies . . . Equivalence of norms needs to be recognised, whether financial, economic, social or environmental. We have lived in a world where the financial and commercial rules fix the general framework. Today we have to re-balance the system. Financial norms should be instruments,

---

11 Even the UN showed its relative impotence in managing the Copenhagen Conference on climate change (only 193 states were represented).

while social and environmental norms are objectives (2010).

In this respect, the rise in significance of the question of fundamental human rights, as much at the international as the European level, has consequences for the evolution of national rights. Their recognition can constitute a limit, admittedly fragile but still real, to the most dangerous practices of neoliberalism.[12]

To follow this path of the re-balancing of norms, an initial imperative to consider with all urgency is the reform of the international monetary system. Its fundamental objective must be to establish currency as a common good of humanity.

A. *Currency as a Common Good of Humanity*

The stake, eventually, of the construction of an international currency is to smash the financial speculation which is, in great part, built on derivatives and therefore on the liberalization of the financial sphere. It is one of the two greatest plagues that currently threaten the world economy. The propositions of the G20 regarding financial regulation are far too modest. This volume proposes, therefore, the principles and stages of the construction of this new currency.

At the time of the four most recent meetings of the G20, the principal decisions taken by the heads of state concerned the actual funds of banks, the tax havens, the bonuses distributed in banks, the governance of the IMF and the organization of the derivatives markets. On the other hand, the role of hedge funds, rating agencies and short sales, while implicated through the financial crisis, were not part of the agenda.[13]

---

12 On this subject, see Marie-Ange Moreau (2006).

Yet, the revision of bank norms when it came to capital stock had been regularly invoked at the time of these meetings. And this revision, considered the principal measure, was the object of a particularly violent counter-attack by the international bank lobby at the last meeting in Toronto.[14] This lobby indicated that the expected measures might notably cost 4 points of growth in Europe from now until 2015, but also 700 billion in capital stock and 5,400 billion in debts in order to strengthen the ratios of solvency and liquidity of the banks from now until 2012. As for the derivatives markets—which will be more organized with the putting in place of a clearing house (Clause 17 of the Pittsburgh Communiqué)—it was not at all a question of limiting their field of operations or, a fortiori, of prohibiting them.[15]

---

13 On these questions, there is currently a conflict between the European parliament and the various governments about regulation of hedge funds (the stake: the European passport which France and other countries refuse to have); on short sales (France and Germany for prohibition, England against); on the prohibition of the most risky financial products without passing through national supervision. Yet, agreement does exist about the framing of bonuses (a limited signal on the stabilization of the financial system), on registration and on a greater transparency of rating agencies. On hedge funds, three problems have been clearly identified: their excess of leverage, which leads to systemic risk; their opacity; and the unbalanced character of relations between hedge funds and investors. It is therefore necessary to put in place a direct regulation of these speculative funds with a limitation of leverage and requirements in terms of liquidity.

14 This was expressed through the International Institute of Finance (that is, of 400 banks in the world). See *Le Monde*, 11, 12 June 2010.

15 One idea would, however, have authorized purchases of CDS only by investors who were owners of sovereign debts, which would have

On the matter of the governance of the IMF, the anticipation was to revise the distribution of voting rights in the limit of 5 per cent (Clause 19 of the Pittsburgh Communiqué). One might wonder about the reasons for such a limitation, which can only go against a genuine political legitimation of the institution.

Finally, running on from these meetings, the American reform, adopted in 2010, led to some advances but they were, in the end, rather modest.[16] In fact, it foresaw the prevention of systemic risk by the commissioning of a financial watchdog committee to identify the institutions considered as bearers of systemic risk. This committee would be able to demand that its capital stock should be strengthened.[17] It was then anticipated that those institutions 'too big to fail' should be dismantled but only when threatened by bankruptcy.[18] Finally, the banks were asked to limit speculative activities—commercial banks could no longer exercise trading activities for their own account and should not hold more than 3 per cent of a speculative fund or a capital investment fund (a rule inspired by Paul Volcker, former chairman of the Federal Reserve).

been a lesser evil. But it was rejected on the grounds that such a verification would be too complicated.

16 Reform of the financial system of 15 July 2010, with the so-called 'Dood-Frank' accord (from the name of the two principal drafters).

17 Let us note that 35 institutions possess assets amounting to more than $50 billion.

18 Of course, it was necessary to go towards a Glass-Steagall, with the separation of bank activities as concerned with deposits (commercial banks) and investment banks. On this point, we are in agreement with the recent declarations of Jacques Cheminade which are available on his website, www.solidariteetprogres.org

TO ACT

But this was not at all a question of prohibiting these activities, since these very banks could develop them on behalf of their clients and earn substantial commissions. In this respect, the American banks began to commit themselves along this path.[19]

But what is most important in respect of the international summits that are today trying to find solutions to the crisis is their refusal to embark upon a reform of the international monetary system. Nevertheless, countries like China, Brazil, Russia and many others[20] want to see this situation itemized on the agenda of these meetings. But each time the refusal has come from the American authorities without the slightest explanation being given. In reality, their attitude is easy to understand. The Americans consider that an international currency already exists and that a reform of the monetary system would very clearly undermine the current status of the dollar.

For their part, the Chinese advocate this reform because the largest share of the reserves of the Central Bank of China is denominated in dollars, and any deterioration of the American currency in relation to others reduces their value. An international currency resting on a basket of currencies would limit the risks of a severe depreciation of reserves and at the same time reduce Chinese dependency in relation to the United States. In addition, the Americans benefit from

19 For details, see *Le Monde*, 24 August 2010.

20 The Chinese Central Bank had already, at the end of March 2009, before the G20 gathering in Pittsburgh, called for the adoption of a new international currency to replace the dollar in the system placed under the auspices of the IMF. It did not even take 48 hours for this idea to be immediately rejected by President Obama.

Chinese refinancing of their public debt, and the Chinese make the United States their principal export zone.

Should one not go beyond this play of intersecting interests that, on a geostrategic level, are tied into a balance of terror whose intensity can only increase over the course of time?

This implies the need to think about a monetary utopia consisting of considering currencies to be the common goods of humanity. If the hypertrophy of the current financial sphere holds, essentially, to the deregulation of exchange and interest rates, a global response has to be provided. It is time to imagine international rules about the formation of interest and exchange rates. To put in place a currency that is 'common', but not necessarily a single currency, in stages, would be the most effective way of reducing the financial sphere, fighting against speculations of all sorts and rediscover the fundamentals of economic life in society.

It is therefore necessary to attack the logic that has provoked the emergence of the gigantic boom in derivatives which formed only 20 years ago. Rather than wanting to manage the explosive dynamic of this boom 'efficiently' through clearing houses, as the G20 proposed, it is clear that the evil needs to be eradicated at its root. One needs to reconsider the double movement of liberalization—of exchange and interest rates—that occurred during the 1970s and 80s. It is this double 'deregulation' that needs to be really called into question. It has provoked the emergence of this immense financial industry of the management of risk, and therefore of the coverage of these risks, which is at the heart of the current crisis.

One of the systemic responses to the systemic crisis is therefore of a macro-economic and macro-financial nature.

The true regulation to be constructed is one that will put in place the landmarks of a future international currency, considered then as a common good of humanity.

Another argument in favour of the remaking of the international monetary system is of a theoretical nature and can be supported by Robert Mundell's so-called law of the impossible trinity. He affirmed that an independent monetary policy on the internal level, the free movement of capital on the external level and a fixed exchange rate for one national currency in relation to others cannot be reconciled with one another. There is an incompatibility that makes it necessary to abandon one of the three elements set out above, namely: autonomous monetary policy; freedom of capital movements; or fixed rates of exchange.

An international currency means adopting fixed parities between the major currencies and abandoning either the freedom of capital movements or an autonomous monetary policy. It appears desirable to abandon the freedom of capital movements when one knows how potentially destabilizing the to-and-fro movement of international capital is to productive activity. It then means putting in place an autonomous monetary policy at the level of each country (or union of countries). This will amount to the government fixing interest rates, necessarily taking account of two contradictory imperatives. On the one hand, it will need to determine the general cost of financing long-term investments which will impel it to reduce the rise in interest rates. But, on the other, it will be necessary for it to attract national savings by sufficiently remunerative interest rates, especially in order to finance public deficits.

This theoretical argument makes possible the founding of a perspective of monetary reform. But setting it to work in a practical sense is obviously something quite different. What is needed is to devote time, to set out the stages of an agenda which could be relied upon over several decades. In the immediate future, the principal difficulty would be of a geostrategic nature due, effectively, to the still real (but declining) reign of the dollar standard.

To this theoretical argument of a technical nature should be added another of a social nature. Currency as a social relation needs also to be considered as a collective relation, a collective relation which necessitates the confidence and cooperation of people. This approach reflects institutional conceptions of currency, one of whose interests is to escape the naturalist conception of optimal monetary zones.[21] The mobility of labour makes it possible to re-establish the balance between regions showing deficits and surpluses—the more the opening to international markets is raised, the more it needs to mitigate external shocks through a fixed exchange rate. Diversification equally makes possible the lessening of the effect of these shocks. This views monetary stability only in terms of mobility of labour, of openings to external exchanges and economic diversification.

On the contrary, institutional conceptions stress the instruments that make possible confidence and cooperation: for example, a common budget; an external monetary policy; the supervision of finance; fiscal harmonization; and a unification of public debts. It is necessary to evaluate the strength and stability of a monetary zone in relation to these elements of an

---

21 For more details, see Michel Aglietta (2010).

institutional nature. In this respect, and to the extent that Europe lacks a sovereign political structure representing a common interest, can be measured the causes for the Eurozone's current weakness and the direction in which Europe needs to commit itself to assure a calmer future for its currency.[22]

Let us equally make it clear that the creation of an international currency does not exclude national or local currencies cohabiting with it. Historically, the presence on the same territory of local, national and foreign money has been the rule more often than the reign of a single currency. But at the beginning of any monetary creation there is the function of the measurement of exchange, the unit of account.

It is here that Keynes' idea of the 'bancor' should be reconsidered. This currency, proposed at the Bretton Woods conference in 1944, is a unit of account for national currencies with an exchange rate fixed between them and the bancor (see Skidelsky 2001). In this system, two types of currency can coexist: the Bancor and the national coinage. A clearing house needs to be created to regulate exchanges between countries. The advantage of the clearing house lies in reducing regulatory transactions between two countries in the balance of their exchanges (as an example, the balance of imports and exports). This system would make possible not only the establishment of the commercial surplus and deficit of each country and the operation of their regulations, but also stigmatize those imbalances in one direction or the other. Keynes' proposition,

---

22 Admittedly, the European stabilization funds have been created with resources amounting to €440 billion, ready to react in the last resort. But it is clear that the striking power of these funds remains weak if an economically more important country than Greece defaults.

therefore, would mean establishing a principle of symmetry between the rights of creditors (those with external surplus) and those of debtors (those with external deficit). The rights of the former are not superior to those of the latter.

In the case of structural imbalances in exchanges between countries, the adjustment then materializes through the possibility of a modification of exchange rates. A country in surplus should either revalue its currency or boost its internal demand. For credits as for unpaid debts, countries would have to pay an interest rate. Each of them would then have a strong incentive not to provoke imbalances in their external exchanges. In this mechanism, speculative movements could easily be prohibited.[23]

To sum up. It has today become imperative to reform the international monetary system. If the solution is an international currency which can cause the disappearance of floating interest rates, several stages would no doubt be necessary to achieve it. First of all, if the euro collapses, a European bancor would then allow the preservation of a common currency alongside the national currencies as well as imply a discipline of exchanges that will affect countries with a deficit as much as those with a surplus. The bancor system could then be extended on a planetary scale with a generalized system of fixed rates. This would then be a common currency for all countries. One can immediately see that, in such a system, Wall Street would cease to have any reason to exist, at least

---

23 It is interesting to note that this system makes it possible to imagine a 'European bancor' in the case of the Eurozone vanishing under the pressure of speculative forces following, for example, a currency war between the euro and the dollar.

that part of it which relates to derivatives, and principally those which have underlying exchange rates, interest rates and therefore state borrowings (CDS).

B. *The Coming of an International Fiscality*

Nevertheless, there could not be a common currency without the creation, on a world scale, of a political authority able to guarantee its credibility. The difficulty the European Union has today encountered in its political construction may well be the same tomorrow while attempting to form a world government. The political leap necessary in order to accomplish this could only follow a democratic path, which is the only way to establish an irrefutable legitimacy.

The creation of a world government along with the creation of a common currency would render credible a whole series of propositions, notably in fiscal matters, which until now have arisen from pious wishes. The obvious character of some examples escape no one. Thus it would mean the (finally definitive) abolition of tax havens due to the setting in motion of a process of fiscal harmonization at the planetary level. In the same way and for the same reasons, why would any country retain secret banking? The annulment of the debts of the poorest countries would cease to be an insurmountable question insofar as financial measures to reduce the inequalities of territorial development could much more easily be put in place.

Although more and more respected voices are currently proposing to tax 'financial transactions', repeating as they do James Tobin's idea of prescribing international financial deals, it is clear that this type of measure could be applied without technical difficulty or major policy.

A quick calculation shows what such a tax could provide if it was applied to financial transactions of any type currently passing through the systems of payment and regulation of the world's central banks (and not only international transactions). This calculation is somewhat particular since it assumes the maintenance of the current system of transactions in derivatives (which moreover one would like to abolish). But by using data from the Bank for International Settlements, Chapter 1 demonstrated how the amount of these transactions had risen by the end of 2007 to around 3,500T$, of which a little less than 1.6 per cent represented transactions in the real economy (54.3 trillion dollars for the world GDP).

A tax of one in one thousand would then represent $3,500 billion a year. A considerable amount, enough at a rough estimate, for example, to audit the world public debt within 12 or 13 years, if this resource was entirely allocated to deal with it. But obviously this tax could, with the mechanisms of redistribution for the poorest countries, also be assigned to the energy and environmental (climate change) challenges facing our planet. A fair return of things which depends only on the political will, in the face of a once more all-powerful globalized finance.

C. *To Raise the Environmental Challenges*

Recent events allow another lesson to be drawn—it will soon be necessary to articulate the agenda for a new financial regulation, one that will emerge from the post-Wall Street world, and the agenda of discussions post-Kyoto and Copenhagen. If there are several aspects manifest in it, the crisis is fundamentally 'one'. To regulate the quantity of carbon emissions;[24] to encourage the development of alternative solutions in matters of energy; and allow China, like other emerging nations, to regulate their emissions—these are of necessity.[25]

The energy- and climate-change challenges impose a profound shift on our societies. Our technical system needs to be transformed and new ways of organizing our towns and our territories need to be invented. Solutions need to be sought for a lasting urbanism: to control energy consuming buildings;[26] diversify modes of transport, productive constructions of energy; and to promote the hydrogen engine.

In order to limit climatic changes and their consequences, some countries have defined policies for controlling emissions of greenhouse gases. These policies are inspired by the principle that 'the polluter is the one who pays'. These countries define a ceiling of emissions (a quota) as well as the objective of a reduction over time. This policy of constraints is associated with market mechanisms to allocate the resources of the carbon economy: an organized market in the buying and selling of emission rights (in the case of over- or under-capacity of emissions by an actor); and a market in coverage products to protect the price in the future, or to make a profit from what is anticipated. There exist several regulatory frames for

24 The objective is eventually to transform CO_2 into chalk, as a series of studies have shown. On this point, see Claude Allègre (2010: 270).

25 The issue is not about 'restructuring' capitalism but 'To know if we can go beyond a system founded on the indefinite accumulation and limitless destruction of nature. Turning towards an "environmental" economy risks being nothing but the capitalist project painted green . . . it is no longer a matter of restructuring, but of going beyond, of thinking in a different way' (Dostaler and Maris 2009: 140).

26 Industrial habitats and premises consume nearly 50 per cent of our energy.

this new organization, founded either on international treaties or private law contracts. Systems of the exchange of rights to emit have been defined at the heart of each regulatory frame—these are the organized markets of 'carbon finance'.

But this system has spiralled out of control. The over-generous distribution of quotas has allowed businesses to get used to a system of emission exchange without immediately being subject to enormous constraint. Businesses have had no difficulty in finding cheap emission rights, which therefore hardly provide an incentive. An oft-invoked track is to anticipate a draconian regulation of carbon finance: the objectives of reduction by 40 per cent of quotas between now and 2020, instead of 20 per cent; the introduction of a minimum price, or even the prohibition of derivatives. All of this looks too much like sloganeering and hardly seems realizable.

The suppression of the market in quotas[27] represents another solution. It would eliminate fears of seeing finance take hold of the climate as it has nevertheless begun to do with derivatives founded on climatic volatility. Now this financial regulation takes place outside of all environmental exigencies and all justice. The suppression of the market in quotas is therefore indispensable. It could only lead to the creation of a carbon tax placed on the whole of exchanges of goods and services which would be different from a single carbon tax at frontiers. What is produced by this tax could finance the ecological transition of our societies through innovative policies in the service of the common good of humanity which the environment has become.

---

[27] According to an idea upheld by Michel Rocard. See also Maxime Combes (2010).

In this transition, it is also necessary to accelerate, at another level, the interconnections of international research in matters of biodiversity (with the Intergovernmental Science-Policy Platform on Biodiversity and Ecosystem Services (IPBES), in process of creation under the auspices of the UN). It is no longer possible to dissociate the future of our societies and our environment from the development of biodiversity.

The opportunity would thus present itself to show that other public policies are possible to build the social, ecological and democratic planet that we need now more than ever.

An Economic Integration of the Major Regions of the World

Our vision of what our planet could be without Wall Street is worldwide and assumes a long gestation, even if, at a given moment, a rupture in the current logics appears inevitable. Must we fear, then, that the world will be reorganized on a regional basis and give in, on this scale, to the temptation for protectionism? Must we then say, as some do, that if so the worst is still to come?

On the contrary, a multipolar and multilateral world could be the middle path for the organization of the planet, on condition that it is not opposed, according to the well-understood principle of subsidiarity, to the formation in parallel (or subsequently) of a world government. In effect, it is necessary to defend the idea that large-scale continental blocks, for example Europe, Latin America, South-East Asia and so on, can be factors for peace and security on our planet.

It is at this level of the organization of economic integration that customs unions could be established to avoid the calamity of wage competition on the international level. And extending integration one notch, these economic zones could also function as a monetary union with mechanisms of budgetary coordination which could be progressively put in place.[28] The attempts that are currently extant in Latin America have already been discussed. This is only the beginning of an embryonic process but one moving in the right direction.

The framework thus created will be ideal to regulate international commerce in other ways, by limiting or prohibiting certain productions and taxing imports depending on social and environmental factors. Naturally, these measures of effective mechanisms will need to be accompanied by international solidarity to avoid continental disequilibrium. But it would offer a real means by which to relocalize the economy over these vast ensembles.

For the regions and countries of the South, this will equally contain, over these vast ensembles, margins for changing internal policies, in a direction that will allow the reduction of major imbalances and inequalities, and a means of advancing democracy.

Thus, the establishment of regional alliances, on a basis not of competitiveness but of complementarity and solidarity, the creation of regional currencies—in short, the establishment of multipolar centres that are truly integrated economically and (why not) politically (as Europe is currently trying to do, admittedly with difficulty)—could be a source of renewal and dynamism for the entire planet. An accompaniment by renewed and decentralized worldwide institutions by major regions would constitute a supplementary advantage.

---

28 While moving in this direction, Europe has not yet experienced this sort of integration.

The Creation of Public Financial Centres
and the In-depth Rehabilitation of Public Services

One of the effects of the financial crisis in the developed countries has been the multiplication, by states, of financial acquisition of stakes in bank capital or their nationalization. Most of the time this has involved very large banks. One would have thought that this public presence at the heart of these banks would have represented a genuine opportunity to institute a different policy by which to finance the economy. This has, however, not been the case, because the banks have very often reimbursed what they considered to be advances. Countries have thereby lost an opportunity to create public financial centres, functioning as long-term investors.

Indeed a financing of projects in the most vital sectors of the economy, which could take 20 or 30 years to come to a conclusion, should not await private investors and financial markets. From a perspective of sustainable development, public financial poles will be a considerable contribution to promote, on a grand scale, financial interdependence, equitable commerce and, especially, renewable energy.

Here again, we may fear that we will have to wait for the next great financial crisis (which could be soon) before civilian and political awareness is able to begin to fix the necessity entirely to revise the financing circuits of the economy into their projects. It is not about nationalizing all credit, or of nationalizing all the largest banks. What is really at stake today is, above all, the mastery by governments of the financing of the economy in the long and very long term, and especially the financing of energy infrastructures.

In order to control the financing circuits, the formulae can be diverse, going from acquiring a stake in bank capital to the pure and simple nationalization of some of them or of taking measures to frame credit fiscally so that it favours this type of investment. It is, in fact, a question of contributing to the financing of collective goods, some of which are the common goods of humanity like energy and the future of the climate, at the level of each nation. In order to finance these common goods, each nation will need to show that it is prepared to cooperate with others in having a respect for a principle of subsidiarity.

The actions of the state in financial matters must equally concern its own domains. It needs in particular to restore public services and renew investment in them. The 40 years of neoliberalism have, at times, created considerable havoc in certain sectors. This is why it is necessary to privilege anew and in an absolute way the use-value of goods which have a genuinely collective sense and not their exchange value. This recognition should entail the prohibition of all commercialization concerning them.

This intransigent attitude needs particularly to be the case for those elements that are indispensable to life: seeds; water; health; education; but also life-long education, research and so on. It is for each nation to favour, for example, plans for the reduction of the use of pesticides or the creation of natural parks.

At the Local Level,
Short Circuits of Production and Distribution

Movements favouring the relocalization of economic activities are multiplying across the world. The idea can be expressed simply—production needs to take place where we consume it, and be consumed where it is produced. It would be very naive to believe that this is a question of simple transfers of economic activities or simple relocalizations. The perspective is a lot more ambitious, and is about favouring decentralized *and* horizontal local cooperation, through networks distributed in such a way that people may together reappropriate the creation of things, which would then be available for them and everyone, if they so wish. The aim being to sustain common goods and common production as much as possible so as to weaken dependency upon the market economy.

This local framework is propitious for multiple complementary actions which, in one way or another, amount to protecting local ecosystems. This protection is necessary if we want to again find lasting modes of production and not be subject to the logic of ever greater production without taking into account the negative externalities that might follow from it. Rediscovering local ecosystems means, for example, stemming the disappearance of bees, perpetuating natural patrimonies, preserving threatened species and protecting rivers.

To aid and facilitate this sort of action, a finance of proximity, represented often as 'solidarity' finance, has developed to some extent everywhere in the world. This gathers together not only options like microcredit or microfinance but also movements which militate in favour of local currency, conceived as a currency that is complementary to the national one.

Solidarity finance, like local finance, renders possible economic ideas with a strong social utility, thereby contributing to lasting and local development. At the same time, through its very close knowledge of territories, solidarity finance is an efficient weapon in the struggle against exclusion and contributes in a major way to social cohesion.

One of the pillars of solidarity finance is microcredit. This consists in the allocation of small-scale loans to people who have no access to classic bank loans. Microcredit has proliferated over five continents and has a total of 150 million borrowers.[29] It has given birth to other microfinance services. The number of institutions of microfinance in the world oriented to the ends of solidarity is estimated at 10,000 (IMF). There equally exist intermediaries who bring financial means to the IMF (Sidi, Oikocredit, Babyloan, La Cofides, Garrigue).[30]

Another form of solidarity finance is the American mechanism of the Community Reinvestment Act (CRA).[31] This plan forces American banks to place a large part of their deposits in the territories where they have been collected, notably in difficult quarters, alongside disadvantaged communities.

Let us, at the same time, evoke the role of local currencies as the source of the regeneration of the local fabric. This type of experience is multiplying at present. Consider the example of the communitarian bank Palmas, co-founded in 1998 by

---

29 Is microcredit too expensive? A lot of detractors think so. In reality, when one looks at the programmes of training and accompaniment linked to it, on the one hand one sees that average interest rates in the world (32 per cent three years ago), have been brought down (26 per cent in 2009). On the other hand, usury rates can reach 100–300 per cent. And in 40 developing countries, local banks often lend at even higher rates. One can therefore understand the current extension of microcredit in the world.

30 The social and interdependent economy is described in Anglo-Saxon countries by the term 'social business' or the third sector.

31 See the instructive interview with Claude Alphandéry (2010/11).

Joaquim Melo in a Brazilian favela. It issues its own currency (the palma)[32] and its avowed aim is to contribute to the relocalization of the economy: 'We are still poor, not only because we don't have much money but especially because we spend it outside the favela. To emerge from poverty, we need as far as possible to produce and consume on the spot'. This implies the creation of a made-to-measure tool, the communitarian bank which issues its own money. The bank's objective is therefore to relocalize the economy and generate wealth on the spot by means of a social currency that has parity with the Brazilian real. With the success of this operation, the founder decided in 2003 to create an institute charged with making the methods of the bank known and promoted.[33]

If, in a general way, the financial crisis has spared solidarity finance, since the latter is not directly linked to the functioning of finance markets, it has on the other hand suffered its effects by reason of the rise in unemployment and the deepening of inequalities.

But must we, for all that, believe that solidarity finance is an aid allowing us to emerge from the crisis?[34] It has admittedly served transformation in depth of local society, but can we be confident that it could, on its own, revolutionize the current financial system? We have already explained why we

32 See *Le Monde*, 'Economie: spécial Économie sociale et solidaire' (26 May 2010), and Joaquim Melo et al. (2009).

33 On a completely different continent, the European reference in matters of microfinance is the Italian Banca Etica, because it brings together this diversity while trying to begin from the savings of a given territory in order to finance social projects with social or ecological ends addressed to a priority population.

34 See Alphandéry (2010/11).

do not intend to fall into responses of the 'localized' type—they may appear attractive but are in the end rather naive with respect to the power relations and the interests at play at the planetary level.

On the other hand, the values that solidarity finance conveys are essential for preparing the ground for the changes we expect. These values are patience, long-term thinking, risk sharing and, finally, ideas that create social links and aid living.

The will to relocalize economic activities, thanks especially to solidarity finance, is today an essential element of the change to which we need to commit ourselves. But this movement does not attack one of the major wounds of our economic system—the current organization of businesses, the majority of which are subject today to a financial pressure that has become intolerable in spite of the crisis.

TO CHANGE FINANCIAL LOGIC:
RECASTING PROPERTY RIGHTS

In the previous chapter I wanted to grapple with the danger of shareholder value, the other great cancer eating away at the core of the world economy. The battle that needs to be undertaken against this disease again justifies the suppression of the financial markets in their present form. In the image of Wall Street, these markets are the active propagators of shareholder value through the actions of the largest financial investors. In only about 20 years, this establishment of a value for the benefit of financial shareholders has exercised a pressure at the core of what is considered to be the heart of capitalism—the joint stock companies. The companies which assume this juridical form, especially those quoted on the stock exchange, are now forced to satisfy the appetite of shareholders in a proportion that is clearly insane.

It is imperative to make a break with the financial logic of shareholder value in the short term if we are to avoid the considerable damage this logic has entailed for the world of work.

The stock exchange of shares is the ideal way to make companies pay the cost of their capital stock—in other words, what the return to shareholders as recompense for their contributions should be. But, as the shareholders have at their disposal not only the privilege of deciding how the profits from the business are allocated but also of nominating the administrators of the company, there is no a priori limit to the proportion of the results they can pay to themselves.[1] Especially when they have conditions of financial profitability fixed a priori and which are imposed universally on the activity of the business. In order to change the current logic of how business results are shared, a central and particularly sensitive question, the intervention of the public powers and the legislator proves to be indispensable.

In this field, alternative tracks are few and all are either difficult or radical. I have identified three. The first may be to take a step back and impose some profound modifications in the legislation concerning pension and retirement funds through capitalization. The second, to consider a rapid and much broader development of the social and solidarity economy. But is such a path really conceivable? The third would be a change in the rules of governance and of property rights in joint stock companies. But would this be a new utopia?

Let me immediately make my position clear about these three solutions. It would seem almost impossible to put the first actually into practice given the current financial logic. The second is eminently desirable but will long remain

---

[1] It is not rare for companies to pay to their shareholders dividends that go beyond the benefits of the exercise. It is enough for that to dip into the company funds!

marginal, even with renewed logics. The third is most effective and quickest to put in place but also undoubtedly the most radical. Indeed, it touches on the very foundation of property rights in joint stock companies.

I will therefore insist principally on the second and third paths which alone will allow the construction of a new world without Wall Street.

ONE. 'TAKING A STEP BACK'

Is it possible to take a step back? To do so the financial norm imposed on businesses when they have recourse to 'highly professional' financial investors (that is, those who, in reality, very effectively set the conditions of profitability for their contributions) would have to be abolished. These conditions fixed a priori have been disastrous and have for 20 years or more modified the traditional logic of capitalism. This logic was once that of the maximization of profit. Now the system in its entirety has begun to come off the rails due to the fact that the obligation of means, namely making the maximum profit, has been transformed into an obligation of result in order to respond to a norm fixed a priori.

Should we take a step back? This would mean relocating traditional logics in which the maximization of profit would imply recognition by managers of the *constraints* their action could encounter. This *maximization under constraints* could justify social compromises which were, for example, appropriate in the post-war Fordist period. Such a step back, even if it could appear to some people as eminently desirable, appears in reality to be extremely difficult to effect for two kinds of reasons.

The first is that of the growing weakness of collective negotiation and the increasing loss of influence by the trade unions. Where have the great social compromises of yesteryear gone? Do we see general strikes that last more than a day? Who can therefore believe in the real effectiveness of trade union actions of a national character (demonstrations, days of action, strikes and so on)? They have almost vanished, replaced by local, detached conflicts in which everyone is trying to conserve their jobs as best they can and often in the worst of conditions. And when their jobs vanish, the only possible demand the work force has is to negotiate redundancy terms.

The solution to the financialization of the economy can therefore no longer come from this world. Global finance, through its powerful bank oligopoly, has taken hold of the world of business and contributed to the progressive destruction of any form of effective opposition force, especially anything which could result from collective negotiation. Is it possible to take this route again? We do not believe so as long as the power of the oligopoly is maintained.

A similar reasoning can be applied to another great actor of social transformations—the state. This is the second reason that impels us to believe in the impossibility of stepping back.

The weakness of states when confronted with the crisis is the best example of this. Not only did governments (motivated by their neoliberal ideology) not see the crisis coming, but also the solutions they have progressively put in place in order to emerge from it have very largely been inspired by the international bankers' lobby. The supreme *tour de force* on the part of banks has been to convince governments to transform their private over-indebtedness (due to the toxic assets linked to the sub-primes) into a public over-indebtedness! It might have been possible to imagine solutions for the restructuring of the public debt (especially that of Greece), but all of them have been rejected. It was naturally necessary to avoid the results of the largest banks being affected by such a plan.

Can we then imagine (in the current context) governments reining in the crazy demands of globalized finance? As yet there is no indication of their attempting to do so. None of the last four G20 communiqués, detailed as they were, made mention of the question of shareholder value and the impossible demands it makes upon the business world.

Why this silence? We think that for governments to address this problem would mean challenging the rights of shareholders to decide on the sharing of the profits of the business. In other words, it would fundamentally challenge the property relations that have until now forged the countenance of capitalism. Admittedly, the world can now see how the irruption of institutional investors has changed the nature of the capitalist enterprise by radically modifying its traditional objectives. This perversion of the system, which is new, does not however touch the juridical shape of the joint stock company. This is where the contradiction lies. It is one that is insurmountable for our current political leaders. If governments want to recover the margins necessary for any political action, they will need to overcome this contradiction.

TWO. THE REINFORCEMENT OF THE SOCIAL
AND SOLIDARITY ECONOMY

The idea being defended here is at once that of the necessary reinforcement of the field of social and solidarity economy, but also of the help that should be brought to this economy so that it recovers, as quickly as possible, its ethical fundamentals.

Traditionally, the domain of the social economy is of associations, mutual societies, cooperatives and foundations. But, with the globalization and financialization of the economy, this field has lost part of its benchmarks. More recently, a change has occurred bringing renewal. A throng of scattered but daring initiatives, like local government councils, parental crèches, equitable exchange, social entrepreneurship[2] and so on have been added to the traditional field. These new spaces for initiative return to the notion of a 'solidarity' economy which has made its presence felt of late. In a certain way, this new economy is in the process of rebuilding the essence of the cooperative movement. It is this movement and the renewal it represents that, during the current period, can become a space for the redeployment of economic activities which follow the logics of social proximity and innovation.

The cooperative movement was fully constituted at the time of the Industrial Revolution following the second enclosures movement in England, and then in France in reaction to the rise of the wage-earning class.[3] Cooperative associations were then created in Europe with the aim of working together rather than entering into competition. They were in some way centres of resistance in which the principles

---

2 The ultimate aim of social entrepreneurship is to replace humans at the centre of the economy with a more reasonable search for profit. For some years, chairs in social entrepreneurship have been opened in Oxford, at HEC, Paris, and at ESSEC.

3 The enclosure movement refers to the expropriation of lands for collective use, which unfolded over several centuries and preceded and prepared the way for the Industrial Revolution.

of a different form of organization from those of capitalism were announced from the very beginning. Thus the principle of 'one man–one vote' and of 'indivisible reserves' emerged from it with, as the key theoretical reflection round the concept of collective property.

As time passed, these principles were eroded under the effects of an increasing porosity with the competitive sector of the economy and the difficulty of adapting to globalization. From the 1970s, with the competition with massive distribution companies in particular, with their financial resources and technical superiority, the cooperative sector sought to popularize itself. In particular, it mimicked the private sector in its forms of organization, at times even penetrated it (for example, with the creation of shared branches). But the entryism of capitalism could be still more direct when the parent societies with cooperative status created branches with 100 per cent holdings with employees who did not have the status of cooperators. For their part, mutual societies, in banking or insurance especially, have seen their activities framed, if not annexed, by governments in a move towards the institutionalization of their status.

Due to the hold of globalized and liberalized finance on the sphere of economic activities, one can observe a renewal in the cooperative movement and a return of its founding values. The social and solidarity economy has since then been established as 'the capacity for collective care by a population over a given territory of the businesses which concern it'.[4]

---

4 See Jacques Prades (2006). To illustrate this argument, the author gives three examples: the Basque cooperative group Mondragon (Spain); the corporation of communitarian economics in Montreal; and the Italian Banca Etica.

This happens through the creation of collective ownership and in such a way as to allow people to take their affairs in hand. The ideas of rootedness within a territory, of social innovation and of direct democracy constitute the keywords of this renewal.

It is this economy that needs to be promoted, that should be encouraged and developed. This represents an essential political responsibility that has to be assumed at every level of public activity. The diversity of forms of solidarity cooperatives and initiatives must be encouraged for they present a proximity with diverse organisms of solidarity finance. Housing cooperatives take part in the struggle for the right to have a home, cooperatives of local services are involved in the right to work, just as credit cooperatives are involved in the right to economic initiative.

This reappropriation of social space becomes an essential stake for the future of our societies. The fact of counting on its strengths, of taking control of its life, of creating collectives founded on the heterogeneity of groups and not on their homogeneity, of fighting against exclusion, is in the end the surpassing of the individual. Of course, it is obviously not a matter of denying the individual but, on the contrary, of the individual being projected into a place where a sense of utopia and the collective imagination may be discovered. We are, now, far from the completely financialized 'radiant' future promised by Wall Street.

THREE. NEW PROPERTY RELATIONS
IN JOINT STOCK COMPANIES

The development of the social and solidarity economy is obviously an essential orientation for the development of our societies. But is this the only true solution? Perhaps not. Its strong territorial anchorage, its organizations on a human scale, its symbolic and practical distance from the wage earners make the social economy a sector unable to respond to all of the productive projects required by the planet. What is more, there is a great need to emerge from the reality of the current economic system in which the great majority of the production of goods and services is realized in medium- or large- size businesses, employing up to tens of thousands of employees.

Unlike the cooperative sector, these are businesses that submit to the yoke of shareholder sovereignty and that, consequently, are subject to a financial pressure which has today become intolerable, especially for the world of work. Legally, these businesses are joint stock companies, very often organized in groups of societies united by capitalistic links. Corporate law organizes power relations at the heart of these sometimes very complex wholes. Concretely it is the shareholders, especially those of the parent company, that hold the ultimate reality of power.

Shareholders possess two types of essential prerogatives. One, by naming the administrators they hold key to how the business is organized. Two, by deciding how the profit is to be divided they control what their contributions are to earn (dividends), and the ways in which they intend to assure the future of the society (investments). In some legislations, one part of the profit can be reserved for the employees.

But the irruption of shareholder value within the recent history of capitalism has fundamentally perverted the traditional logic of the power relations at the heart of capitalist business. An infernal logic has thereby been installed, and current company law cannot absolutely contain it since it is precisely these rights that rest in the ultimate power of the shareholder—of the one who brings capital (one share–one voice).

The question here is: How can this insane logic, largely propagated by the financial markets by allowing institutional investors and the banks that manage their funds to disseminate this virus, be torn to shreds?

Paradoxically one can take as a point of departure a proposition by French President Nicholas Sarkozy. Faced with the extent of the crisis and the problems of purchasing power, he brought together on 18 February 2010 the social partners and said he was favourable to the rule of three-thirds in profitsharing: one third for investments, one third for shareholders, one third for staff. Simultaneously, to clear the way, especially the resolute opposition of the French employers, he entrusted a mission to analyze this subject to the director general of INSEE. In spite of everything, his wish was for an agreement between the social partners on a rule of equal shares rather than to put a law in force.

Presented as such, this proposition was not even an impossible undertaking. It is entirely contradictory with regard to the current rules of governance of joint stock companies. In contrast, if it is a matter of 'restructuring capitalism', another presidential formula, or better, of finding new paths (alternative ones) in the organizational and functional logics of companies, the setting up of a rule of equal shares could then become a point of departure.

A rule that would impose, by law, the dividing of the results in three parts would take away from the shareholders one of the essential attributes of their power. It would remove the lever that allows them to carry out strategic arbitrations between the past (in other words, remuneration by dividends on funds provided) and the future (the funds which would be destined for investments, the generators of future results). To withdraw this fundamental power from shareholders would be to destroy the logic of strategic decision-making of the capitalist company, whether traditional or financialized, but without for all that setting up a form of governance that could deal with the new conditions of division.

Moreover, for the company subject to shareholder value, in order to guarantee the shareholders their remuneration, two complementary plans have been introduced into its governance. On the one hand, independent administrators on the board to exercise, if necessary, opposition to the management (and thereby prevent it from 'taking root' or acting on its own account). On the other hand, stock options as well as bonuses for the directors, the objective of which is narrowly to align their interests with those of the shareholders.

From that time, the sharing of the results is made under the following conditions: one part for dividends, another for the self-financing of the investments, but with two additions. The general assembly of shareholders decides the allocation of stock-options to the leading executives, and the board determines the amount of the directors' bonuses through the remuneration committee. There again, the shareholders of these particular companies, since they are subject to share-holder value, have complete power over the rule of equal shares while playing this time on several of the organs of governance. The edifice of this power is therefore now a lot more sophisticated and complex but also probably more fragile. A rule of three-thirds, imposed from the outside, could obviously only destroy it.

Another solution would simply be for power between opposing actors to be shared. In this hypothesis, how should organs of governance be conceived in relation to the setting up of a new rule of equal shares? Is it possible to have a company which would be neither a joint stock company nor a cooperative company but which would be a credible alternative for the organization and management of economic activities? A company that combines one rule for the providers of capital (one share–one vote) and one rule for the providers of the work force (one man/woman–one voice)?

This must be answered in a way that will not be a 'restructuring of capitalism but a pathway which branches off to offer a new vision. Such a new company may be called an 'alternative partnership business',[5] whose objective will be the sharing of power and the negotiation of the results between the providers of funds, the directors and the workforce. The standard results after taxes could remunerate the past (those who provided funds), the present (the workforce and the directors) and the future (the investments). This sharing is justified by the risk taking of each of those involved. The orientations and the profile of the organs of governance , along with the distribution of property rights in this new business, may be as follows:

---

5 Economists often make a distinction between a stakeholder business, in which those actively involved (workforce, bankers, clients) play a role in the decision making, and the second, called a shareholder business, where the shareholders assert their authority when it comes to decision-making. But these two categories of company, and especially the stakeholder business, remain within the logic of 'joint stock company' functioning. The alternative partnership business does not therefore refer to this distinction.

The board would, above all, be a genuine administration board of 'time', in the sense that it should make strategic arbitrations between:

- the remuneration of those who, *in the past*, have provided funds; this should be sufficient for the providers not to sell off their shares but to continue to feed their funds into the company;

- the remuneration of those who, *in the present*, have guaranteed, through their work, the realization of the company's activities and its results. It is necessary from this point of view to able to consider the skills of each person, especially that of the directors. On condition, however, that these different remunerations result from a transparent decision taken by the board (this clearly does not concern salaries that continue to be fixed through collective bargaining);

- the financing of the investments which prepare and condition the *future* of the company's activities.

This administration board could be represented equally by its four components. One, the representatives of fund providers—chosen by the providers according to the number of shares held (one share–one vote). Two, the representatives of the workforce—chosen according to the one man (or woman)–one vote principle, by the company's workforce. Three, specialists, especially in the scientific realm, whose role would be to anticipate the future for the medium- or long-term strategic choice of investments and their financing. They would consequently play an important role in the strategic choices of investments and their financing. They would be designated in parity with the representatives of the fund providers and the workforce. Four, the directors of the company. It is tripartite and each body designates one of the branches which constitute it.

What will the balance of powers then be? The chair of the board of directors could be a representative of the capital providers (with a casting vote), while the chair of the management board could be from the workforce (with a casting vote). But the procedure could be reversed according to the nature of the activity and this could be justified, for example, in the case of bank or insurance activities.

After the initial capital stock symbolized by social shares, the appropriate funds will need to be fed each year by part of the current results, that which is destined for investments. This part will be generative of new social shares which are to be allocated to the fund providers, the workforce and the directors pro rata in relation to the rise in the current result distributed to them. The key to the distribution of the current result (after the decisions about investments) will therefore also be that which serves the distribution of the social shares. This key will be decided each year by the board of directors.

This organization of governance will obviously modify the place of shareholders in the company. Nevertheless, the arrangement of powers is ordered in a clear way on the basis of decisions of a strategic type (the board of directors) and those which arise from the day-to-day management (the management board). It avoids all paralysis in its working, whether in the short or the long term. The sharing of powers is realistic, because each of those actively involved can plainly express themselves within their own realm of competence.

A company built on this model has no reason to be afraid of bankers or providers of capital. Its *affectio sociatis* (or common will for several people to associate physically or morally with each other) is by nature raised. In the same way, it can be conceived that the work of the employees will not be subject to pressure from any of the parties involved, but will be considered as making an essential contribution to the company's life. Why will such a company need to make an appeal to the financial markets or Wall Street? To do so will be to subject it once more to the financial norm that investors would impose a priori on them.

CONCLUSION

After this scan of the horizon, the question that comes to mind about this new world, a world without Wall Street, is the possibility of such a scenario occurring, and when it might be expected? The response to this double question depends in part on another: What is the likelihood of another wide-ranging systemic crisis? In the first part of this book the idea was developed that a future financial catastrophe is practically inevitable and will probably occur quite soon. This is the profound conviction of many. One of the possible ways out of the crisis can then be a world without Wall Street, but it is not the only one.

In my opinion, the coming crisis will occur for essentially three reasons. One, the countries participating in the G20 meetings have not challenged the madness represented by derivatives linked to financial liberalization. They have barely been able to foresee the best way to organize their markets. Two, the rapidity with which derivatives continue to develop can only portend a fresh crisis—the most worrying sign obviously being the CDS on government borrowings. Three, at no time have the leaders of the developed countries confronted the increasing ravages that shareholder value has wreaked on the world of work.

The future crisis will then be able to play the role of electro-shock therapy that this time risks being fatal, because governments have no room for manoeuvre. What is more, the public has grown weary of empty promises. At stake is undoubtedly the fate of democracy and world peace.

We have seen that the scenario of a 'world without Wall Street' is not the only one possible. After the next financial storm, it is unfortunately possible to imagine worse scenarios. They have been evoked in this book and do not require to be extended further, except for one thing—politicians are loath to evoke the worst paths. To a certain extent this is understandable. But are they not there, one might say that this is their function, to remind us of the radiant roads that await us thanks to their inescapably credible and effective actions?

As for intellectuals and academics, these constraints of analysis and communication do not exist in the same way. Our responsibility is to speak our truth as citizens and express our convictions in the light of our analyses, expertise and experience. To this must be added our doubts and working hypotheses but also the well-founded belief we hold dear. We exist within the realm of the sciences of society, of the human and social sciences, and not in those of the hard sciences. This brings a necessary acceptance of debates of ideas and intellectual pluralism on which we have so insisted.

The key to the change that can lead us into a world described here as 'without Wall Street', is therefore the formulation of a credible project, or, more accurately, of a practical utopia. In this the recommendation formulated recently by Marcel Gauchet in *Le Monde* is being followed: 'A revolution needs a revolutionary programme. We start in the name of a hope, a vision of the future, a feeling that other solutions are close at hand' (19 July 2010).

This project has been developed round a few themes that have seemed to me unavoidable, that of a world government that needs to be formed as soon as possible to tackle the monetary question as a priority, the only path possible to reduce speculative booms that are the cause of the increasing instability of the international financial system and the ever more serious crises that have developed over the past 15 years. But the worldwide level can equally be the level appropriated to treat the question of international taxation in liaison with the financing of the great energy questions that await our planetary environment.

The worldwide approach must also be combined with regional and national approaches. The idea of the economic integration of the largest regions of the world can contribute to peace on our planet. In the same way, the creation of public national financial centres seems to be the right scale at which to resolve a series of problems linked to renewable energy and the financing of public services (that have to be reinforced). Finally, the local level seems absolutely adapted for the setting up of short circuits of production and distribution, in osmosis with the circuits of solidarity finance.

There finally remains, to ease the financial pressure exercised by shareholder value over businesses, a vigorous action by public powers in favour of the social and solidarity economy. This action can be an important, but probably insufficient, initial path to escape the grip of financialization.

Indeed, it is a matter only of an economy of proximity, that cannot be called upon to deal with the fate of large businesses. The more ambitious path, but also the most difficult, passes, as far as we are concerned, through a recasting of corporate law (at least for capitalist societies) by modifying the balances of current powers. This reform would put in place an *alternative partnership form of company*, in which within the organs of governance would simultaneously be combined the cooperative principle (one man or woman–one vote) for the representation of the workforce, and the capitalist principle (one share–one vote) for the representation of the fund providers. The structure of governance (a board of directors of time and a management board) would ensure a coherent hierarchy of decision making to avoid any form of paralysis.

It should be said that the challenges that await our planet are considerable: the challenges of the environment, energy and food, obviously, but also challenges in the monetary order and in that of company property relations. These stakes are so fundamental that they call for new practices at the level of the citizen that would bring meaning, especially for the young, into their relation towards work and money.

Should it not take 'knowing how to share' and 'sharing knowledge' along with, fundamentally, a principle of multi-culturalism in order to be a citizen of the world to come? Is it not a matter of allowing all branches of knowledge, even the traditional ones, all philosophies and cultures, all of the moral and spiritual forces capable of promoting ethics to participate in the construction of alternatives?

Can we not indeed hope that our national, and we hope soon our international, communities would be sufficiently brought together by values and that they would be propelled by concerns so that the economy might finally appear simply as a means? Are these concerns and values not in the end freedom, dignity, security, individual flourishing and collective well-being?

SHARE OF THE REMUNERATION OF WAGE-EARNERS IN THE ADDED VALUE
(TO THE COST OF FACTORS) OF NON-FINANCIAL SOCIETIES.

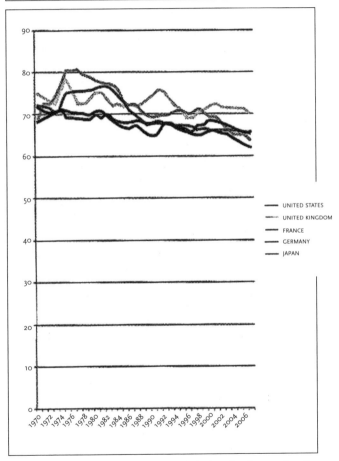

SOURCE: INSEE: Report on the share of added value, the sharing of profits
and the division of remuneration in France, June 2009.

APPENDIX 2

US AND EUROPEAN BANKS	2008
ROYAL BANK OF SCOTLAND	3,550
DEUTSCHE BANK	3,171
BARCLAYS	3,036
BNP PARIBAS	2,988
HSBC	2,582
CRÉDIT AGRICOLE	2,395
JP MORGAN	2,220
UBS	1,948
ING	1,917
BANK OF AMERICA	1,856
SOCIÉTÉ GÉNERALE	1,627
BANCO SANTANDER	1,511
UNICREDIT	1,506
ALLANZ	1,375
CREDIT SUISSE	1,132
AXA	969
DEXIA	937
SAN PAOLO	916
NATIXIS	799
BBCA	780
TOTAL STOCKS	**37,215**

AGLIETTA, Michel. 2010. 'La monnaie est aussi un bien public, générateur de lien social et politique'. *Le Monde Economie*, 1 June.

—— and Antoine Rebérioux. 2004. *La Dérive des marchés financiers.* Paris: Albin Michel.

——, Sabrina Khanniche and Sandra Rigot. 2010. *Hedge Funds: Entrepreneurs ou requins de la finance?* Paris: Perrin.

ALPHANDÉRY, Claude. 2010/11. 'Le baromètre de la finance solidaire'. *Finansol/La Croix*. Available at: www.finansol.org/docs/Barometre-2010-de-la-finance-solidaire.pdf

ALLÈGRE, Claude. 2010. *L'imposture climatique ou la fausse écologie.* Paris: Plon.

Alternatives économiques. 2008. Special crisis issue (November).

AMENC, Noël. 2007. 'Trois premières leçons de la crise de crédits sub-prime'. Nice: EDHEC Risk and Asset, Management Research Centre (August).

ARTUS, Patrick. 2007. *La Liquidité incontôlable. Qui va maîtriser la monnaie mondiale?* Paris: Pearson.

—— and Michèle Denonneuil. 1999. 'Crisis, recherché de rendement et comportements financiers: l'interaction des méchanismes microéconomiques et macroéconomiques'. *L'architecture financière internationale* 18: 55–96.

—— and Marie Paule Virard. 2005. *Le capitalisme est en train de s'autodétruire.* Paris: La Découverte.

—— and Jean-Paul Betbèze, Christian de Boissieu, Gunther Capelle-Blancard. 2008. 'Le crise des subprimes'. Paris: Conseil d'Analyse Économique, p. 23.

AUTORITÉ DES MARCHES FINANCIÈRES (AMF). 2008. 'Une analyse de la notation sur la marché des RMBS «sub-prime» aux États-Unis', *Risques et Tendances* 4 (January).

BAUDRU, Daniel, Stéphanie Lavigne and François Morin. 1999. *Gestion institutionelle et crise financière: un gestion spéculative de risque*. Paris: Conseil d'analyse économique, pp. 151–71.

BIS Quarterly Review. September 2007–September 2009, November 1996. Issues are available in their entirety at www.bis.org/publ/qtrpdf/r_qt1203.htm

BERLIOZ, George. 2008. 'Le capitalisme occidentale entre chocs pétroliers et crise financière'. *La Finance Islamique* (June).

BERNIER, Aurélien. 2010. 'Désobéir pour sortir de l'impasse libérale'. *L'Humanité*, 1 August.

BROSSARD, Olivier. 2001. *Un krach à l'autre: instabilité et régulation des économies monétaires*. Paris: Grasset et Fasquelle.

CAPGEMINI AND MERILL LYNCH. 2008. *Rapport sur la richesse mondiale*. Available at: www.capgemini.com/m/en/n/pdf_Merrill_Lynch_and_Capgemini_Release_12th_Annual_World_Wealth_Report.pdf

CARDONA, Michael and Ingo Fender. 2003. 'L'évolution des facteurs influent sur le comportement des gestionnaires institutionnels: incidence potentielle sur le marché des capitaux'. *Revue de stabilité financière* (June): 98–109.

CARTAPANIS, André. 2008. 'Les *hedge funds* et le risqué systémique' in Bertrand Jacquillat, Jean-Hervé Lorenzi et al, *Hedge funds, private equity, marchés financiers: les frères ennemis?* (Les cahiers du Cercle des économistes). Paris: Presses Universitaires de France.

COMBES, Maxime. 2010. 'La mascarade des quotas de CO2'. *Libération*, 29 April. Available at: www.liberation.fr/societe/0101632633-la-mascarade-des-quotas-de-co2

COMMITTEE OF EUROPEAN SECURITY REGULATORS (CESR). 2008. 'The Role of Credit Rating Agencies in Structured Finance'. Consultation paper (February).

CONSEIL D'ANALYSE ÉCONOMIQUE (CAE). 2003. *Les norms comptables et le monde post-Enron*. Paris.

CONTAMIN, Rémy. 2004. 'Système monétaire international: la logique des inéquilibres'. *Flash Eco,* Crédit agricole (September).

DELLI GATTI, DOMENICO, Gallegatti, Mauro and Gardini Laura. 1994. 'Investment confidence, corporate debt and income fluctuations'. *Journal of Economic Behaviour and Organization* 22: 164–87.

DOSTALER, Gilles. 2000. 'Néolibéralisme, keynésianisme et traditions liberalisme'. *La Pensée* 323: 71–87.

—— and Bernard Maris. 2009. *Capitalisme et pulsion de mort.* Paris: Albin Michel.

DUBOIS, Alain and Jean-Pierre Mustier. 2007. 'Risques et rendement des activités bancaires liées aux Hedge Funds'. *Revue de la stabilité financière* 10 (April).

EUROPEAN COMMUNITIES. 2008. 'The Economics of Ecosystems and Biodiversity'. Available at: ec.europa.eu/environment/ nature/biodiversity/economics/pdf/teeb_report.pdf

FAMA, Éugene. 1965. 'Random Walk in Stock Market Prices'. *Financial Analysts Journal* (September–October).

FENOGLIO, Jérôme. 2010. 'Le triumph et le désastre'. *Le Monde,* 2 August.

FERGUSON Roger and Laster David. 2008. *'Hedge Funds* et risque systémique'. *Revue de la stabilité financière* 10.

GÉNÉREUX, Jacques. 2011. *L'autre société: A la recherche du progrès humain,* revised edition. Paris: Éditions du Seuil.

——. 2009. *Le socialisme néomoderne ou l'avenir de la liberté.* Paris: Éditions du Seuil.

——. 2006. *La Dissocieté.* Paris: Éditions du Seuil.

HANSMANN Henry and Reinier Kraakman. 2002. 'Toward a Single Model of Corporate Law?' in Joseph A. McCahery, Piet Moerland, Theo Raaijmakers and Luc Renneboog (eds), *Corporate Governance Regimes: Convergence and Diversity.* Oxford: Oxford University Press, pp. 56–82.

HOUTART, François. 2008. 'Le monde a besoin d'alternatives et pas seulement regulations.' Available at: www.michelcollon.info/ IMG/article_PDF/article_a1586.pdf

ICART, André. 2000. 'Les banques centrales, la BRI et la stabilité financière'. *Revue française et administration publique* (March).

KENDALL, Maurice George and Austin Bradford Hill. 1953. 'The Analysis of Economic Time-series, Part One: Prices'. *Journal of the Royal Statistical Society*, Series A (General) 16: 11–34.

KONÉ, Solange, Damien Millet, José Mukadi, Ajit Muricken, Victor Nzuzi, Salissou Oubandoma, Aminata Touré Barry, Éric Toussaint and Renaud Vivien. 2008. 'Les resources naturelles, biens communs de l'humanité'. Belgium: Committee for the Abolition of Third World Debt. Available at: www.cadtm.org/Les-ressources-naturelles-biens

KRUGMAN, Paul. 2001. 'Crises: the Next Generation'. *Razin Conference* (March): 25–6.

LORDON, Frédéric. 2010. 'Et si on fermait la Bourse . . .'. *Le Monde diplomatique*, February, pp. 1, 8–9.

LUCAS, Jean-Marc. 2007. BNP Paribas Focus Week, 21 September, pp. 7–36.

McKINNON, Ronald I. 1973. *Money and Capital in Economic Development*. Washington DC: Brooking Institution.

MELO, Joaquim, Élodie Bécu, Carlos de Freitas. 2009. *Viva Favela*. Paris: Michel Lafon, 2009.

MIOTTI, Luis and Dominique Plihon. 2001. 'Libéralisation financière, spéculation et crises bancaires'. *Revue du CEPII* 85 (1st quarter).

MISES, Ludwig von. 1978. *On the Manipulation of Money and Credit*. New York: Free Market Books.

MISHKIN, Frederic S. 1999. 'Lessons from the Asian Crisis'. NBER Working Paper 7102.

MOREAU, Marie-Ange. 2006. *Normes sociales, droit du travail et mondialisation. Confrontations et mutations*. Paris: Dolloz-Sirey.

MORIN, François. 1998. *Le Capitale des grandes entreprises et le restructuration du capitalisme en France. Rapport de mission au ministre de l'Économie, des Finances et de l'Industrie*. Paris: Bercy.

———. 2006. *Le Nouveau Mur de l'argent: Essai sur la finance globalisée*. Paris: Éditions du Seuil.

—— and Lionel Jospin. 2008. 'Faire face à la déraison financière'. *Le Monde*, 6 September.

Payment Systems in Eleven Developed Countries. 1980. Central banks of the Group of Ten countries and Switzerland, under the aegis of the Bank for International Settlements. Available at: www. bis.org/publ/cpss01a.htm

PLIHON, Dominique. 2003. *Le nouveau capitalisme*. Paris: La Découverte.

——. 1999. 'La duperie des fonds de pension; au nom des entreprises'. *Le Monde diplomatique* (February), p. 4.

PRADA, Michel. 2007. 'Le Monde des *Hedge-Funds:* préjugés et realité. La contribution de l'AMF au débat sur les stratégies de gestion alternatives'. *Revue de la stabilité financière* 10 (April).

PRADES, Jacques. 2006. *Compter sur ses propres forces*: *Initiatives solidaires et entreprises sociales*. Paris: l'Aube.

RADURIAU, Geoffroy. 2010. 'Les réseaux de valeur. Une représentation financière et résiliaire des rapports fonds-firmes'. Thesis, University of Toulouse.

RICOL, René. 2008. 'Rapport sur la crise financière'. Mission confié par le Président de la République dans la contexte de la Présidence française de la Union européenne.

ROCHET, Jean-Charles. 2008. 'Le futur de la réglementation bancaire'. *TSE Notes* 2 (December).

SENATE BANKING COMMITTEE. 2007. 'The Role and Impact of Credit Rating Agencies in the Subprime Credit Markets'. *Hearings* (26 September).

SHLEIFER, Andrei and Robert Vishny. 1997. 'The Limits of Arbitrage'. *The Journal of Finance* 52(1) (March): 35–55.

SKIDELSKY, Robert. 2001. *John Maynard Keynes*: *Fighting for Britain, 1937–1946*, VOL. 3. London: Macmillan.

SOMAVIA, Juan. 2010. 'On ne peut se centrer sur les déficits sans mener une politique sociale'. *Le Monde*, 28 May.

SOROS, George. 2008. *The New Paradigm for Financial Markets*: *The Credit Crisis of 2008 and What It Means*. London: Public Affairs.

STANCANELLI, Elena, Guillaume Chevillon, Hélène Baudchon, Gaël Dupont, Amel Falah, Catherine Mathieu, Christine Rifflart, Danielle Schweisguth, Hervé Péléraux, Mathieu Plane, Sabine Le Bayon, Xavier Timbeau, Eric Heyer, Matthieu Lemoine and Paola Veroni. 2005. 'L'axe de croissance. Perspectives 2005–2006 pour l'économie mondiale'. Lettre de l'OFCE (April 2005). Available at: spire.sciences-po.fr/hdl:/2441/2421/resources/260.pdf

STIGLITZ, Joseph E. 1985. 'Credit Markets and the Control of Capital'. *Journal of Money, Credit and Banking*: 133–52.

SUPIOT, Alain. 2010. *L'esprit de Philadelphie: La justice sociale face au marché total*. Paris: Éditions du Seuil.

TIROLE, Jean. 2006. *The Theory of Corporate Finance*. Princeton: Princeton University Press.

———. 2008. 'Leçons d'une crise'. *TSE Notes* 1 (December).

UN. 2010. 'Global Biodiversity Outlook 3' (May). Available at: www.cbd.int/gbo3/

UN WATER, UNEP, FAOWATER. 2010. 'De l'eau propre pour un monde sain', *Journée mondiale de l'eau* (March). Available at: www.unwater.org/wwd10/campaign.html#media

VENDRAMIN, Patricia. 2010. 'Les bouleversements du travail'. *Sciences Humaines* 11 (May–June): pp. 68–9.

WHITE, William R. 2008. 'Past Financial Crises, the Current Financial Turmoil and the Need for a New Macrofinancial Stability Framework'. Presentation at the LSE Financial Markets Group and the Deutsche Bank Conference, 'The Structure of Regulation, Lessons from the Crisis of 2007'. London, 3 March.

WOLF, Martin. 2009. 'Le nouveau plan Obama ne sauvera pas les banques'. *Le Monde*, 17 February.